The
Fishing Hall
of SHAME™

The Fishing Hall of SHAME™

BRUCE NASH and ALLAN ZULLO

Ray Villwock, *Curator*
Bill Maul, *Illustrator*

A DELL TRADE PAPERBACK

A DELL TRADE PAPERBACK
Published by
Dell Publishing
a division of
Bantam Doubleday Dell Publishing Group, Inc.
1540 Broadway
New York, New York 10036

The trademark Dell® is registered in the U.S. Patent and Trademark Office.

The Fishing Hall of SHAME™ is a trademark of Nash & Zullo Productions, Inc.

ISBN: 0-440-50318-3

Text design by Jeremiah B. Lighter

Printed in the United States of America

Published simultaneously in Canada

June 1991

10 9 8 7

RRH

ACKNOWLEDGMENTS

We wish to thank all the professional anglers, guides, charter-boat captains, outdoor writers, game wardens, and weekend fishermen who contributed nominations.

We are especially grateful to those anglers who shared a few laughs with us as they recounted the inglorious moments that earned them a place in The Fishing Hall of SHAME™.

This book couldn't have been completed without the assistance and cooperation of the following: Chris Christian; Bill Cork; Dennis D'Antonio; Ted Dzialo, executive director of the National Freshwater Fishing Hall of Fame; Sugar Ferris, president of Bass'n Gals; Jan Fogt; Tom Hollatz; David Kelly, Library of Congress; Mike Leech, International Game Fish Association; Ann Lewis, of B.A.S.S.; Bob McNally; John E. Phillips; and Bob Smith.

We also extend our thanks to: Jim Barbagallo, Tom Bolinski, Richard Bowles, Jennifer Cardozo, Mary Jane Kayes, George Kremer, Al Lindner, Joe Mullins, Verna Pfarr, Ken Schultz, and Roy Tanaka.

And for steering us clear of all obstacles during this editorial fishing excursion, we thank Sophie Nash, Kathy Zullo, and Judi Villwock.

Contents

The
Fishing Hall
of SHAME™

Casting Off

For years, in our Hall of SHAME™ book series, we have chronicled the wacky, hilarious, embarrassing moments in major sports such as baseball, football, basketball, and golf. But somehow, we managed to overlook America's most popular participatory sport—fishing.

Well, no longer.

From mountain trout streams to pristine bass lakes, from the marlin-rich waters off Hawaii to the tarpon-laden waterways in Florida, we have searched for the funniest, zaniest, incredible-but-true stories in sport fishing.

We combed the archives of the National Freshwater Fishing Hall of Fame in Hayward, Wisconsin, the International Game Fish Association in Fort Lauderdale, Florida, and the Library of Congress in Washington, D.C.

More importantly, we assembled a crack team of outdoor writers who spread out across the country, visiting high-stakes fishing tournaments, back-country fishing holes, ritzy charter-boat marinas, and weather-beaten docks. Our team interviewed boat captains, game wardens, fishing guides, pro anglers, and typical weekend fishermen for their most laughable incidents of ignobility.

Embarrassing moments have happened to them all—even America's most famous fisherman, First Angler George Bush. He suffered the worst case of bluefish blues the world had ever seen when he went seventeen straight agonizing days without hooking so much as a minnow in 1989. President Bush had to resort to prayer before finally catching a fish.

If you've ever pitched overboard or hooked yourself or done something incredibly foolish while fishing, you're not alone. You'll see for yourself in the following pages that pros like Rick Clunn, Guy Eaker, and Zell Rowland have been in the same boat of shame as you have.

Gary Klein, the 1989 Angler of the Year for the Bass Anglers Sportsman Society (B.A.S.S.), confessed that he once put his boat on a high-speed plane through a patch of tall reeds—and wound up in a cow pasture! "At least no one was around to witness this mortifying moment," he said. "But it's okay to tell the story because it's good for a laugh."

Pro angler Jim Bitter relived that sickening moment in 1989 when he committed the costliest fumble in fishing-tournament history. After landing the bass that would have made him a fifty-thousand-dollar winner, Bitter accidentally dropped it over the side—and lost the tourney by a mere two ounces. "That certainly was the most expensive fish I ever lost —and definitely the most embarrassing," said Bitter.

Amateur angler A. Ray Cockrell doesn't talk about the one that got away. He talks about the *ones* that got away. After catching some huge bluefish, he ate one and gave two others away only to find out later that they *all* would have been world records! "I always was astounded whenever I heard stories that someone ate a world-record fish," he said. "I didn't see how it could happen. Now I know firsthand."

Game wardens opened up a treasure trove of crazy fishing "crime stories" for us. Take, for instance, the hefty lady who was nabbed after hiding illegally caught trout in her underwear. Then there was the poor sap who, out of two hundred boats on Lake Erie, picked the one boat that had an off-duty, out-of-uniform wildlife officer and offered him all the over-the-limit fish he had caught!

There have been some painful moments in sport fishing that can't be ignored. Larry Nixon, the all-time leading money-winner on the B.A.S.S. pro fishing circuit, hooked himself in the back of his head with an errant cast.

Ernest Hemingway once was shot in the leg by a shark. And that's no fiction either. The famed author had landed a mako shark on his boat and was going to shoot it when the thrashing mako jostled the trigger. The gun went off and the bullet slammed into Hemingway's calf.

Just what does it mean to be in The Fishing Hall of SHAME™? It's a special recognition of a moment we can all identify with—and laugh about—because each of us has at one time or another screwed up.

FLAIL
TO THE
CHIEF

The Most
Embarrassing
Fishing Misadventures
of U.S. Presidents

George Bush

Off Kennebunkport, Maine, 1989

President George Bush—America's most famous fisherman —suffered the worst case of bluefish blues the world had ever seen.

With an armada of camera boats tailing him on his daily outings off the coast of Maine, the vacationing First Angler went an incredible seventeen straight agonizing, mortifying days without hooking so much as a minnow. And every day that the President returned fishless, the whole world knew.

Finally, with only one full day left to his vacation, a desperate Bush turned to prayer. And it worked. Within an hour after leaving church the President caught a hefty bluefish to put an end to his embarrassing jinx.

In August 1989 Bush had taken his family to their summer home in Kennebunkport, Maine, for a nineteen-day summer vacation. No sooner had he arrived than he hopped into his twenty-eight-foot cigarette fishing boat, *Fidelity,* confident he'd catch some bluefish as he had so many other times before. He didn't mind that a flotilla of press boats was following him to record every moment of his expected angling successes.

Unfortunately, Bush didn't catch a fish that day . . . or the next day . . . or the next . . . or the next. While those around him were getting strikes, the President was striking out—a fact reported daily by the media.

By the tenth day without even a nibble, the Portland, Maine, *Press Herald* began publishing a "fish watch." Every day the paper ran a drawing of a bluefish inside the international symbol for *no* and gave the number of outings the President had gone without catching a fish.

This spurred his staffers into damage control. A White House press official claimed that although Bush hadn't snared any blues yet, several members of the presidential fishing party had caught fish "under the President's very careful tutelage." But the press continued to report his catch of the day: zero.

With only six days left on his vacation, Bush's fishing failures were starting to bug him—especially when he saw White House reporters wearing the *Press Herald*'s "no fish" logo on their press credentials.

With tongue in cheek the President called the logo "a vicious assault on my ability" and threatened to call up the newspaper editors and complain. Then he predicted the slump would end that day because he planned to go out and "murder" some fish. He was even bringing First Lady Barbara Bush with him for good luck.

Barbara's presence did indeed bring good luck—for everyone in the presidential fishing party but her husband. Meanwhile, back on land, some entrepreneurial reporters began selling "no fish" T-shirts to their colleagues.

By now the chagrined President was desperate enough to seek advice from local anglers. Among their recommended strategies were spitting on the bait before casting and using depth charges from one of the Coast Guard vessels that always accompanied him.

As Bush readied his boat for his fifteenth outing, family members tried to buoy his spirits. They chanted, "We want fish!" and "Go for the blues!" Several of his grandchildren held up placards that read, A FISH A DAY KEEPS THE PRESS AWAY, FISH TILL YOU DIE, and GRAMPY, YOU CAN DO IT! Finally, the family serenaded him with an improvised song: "When the Fish Go Marching In."

Despite all their support Bush went fishless again. "It's gotten out of hand," he told the press. "When I see it [his fishing failures] on national television, I know we've got to put an end to this monkey business. So we will prevail. I guarantee you—I positively guarantee you—that this jinx will end."

Reporters nodded and wondered if he would catch a blue in their lifetime. To the President's credit he continued to grin and bear it. However, he did shake his head when White House photographer Dave Valdes simultaneously hooked two bluefish on a line with two sets of triple hooks. And Bush did grit his teeth whenever photographers, in chase boats waiting for him to catch a fish, reeled in bluefish themselves and then held them up for him to see.

On the eighteenth day—the last full day of his summer vacation—Bush sought divine help. He went to St. Ann's Episcopal Church and prayed. "This is it!" Bush told the press as he headed for his final outing. "I can feel it!"

Wearing camouflage pants, an olive drab sweater, a blue

work shirt, and a cap that read USS BLUEFISH, the President roared out into the ocean again with the First Lady and shouted, "We'll stay out for as long as it takes!"

The praying paid off. Using a jawbuster lure Bush landed a two-foot, ten-pound bluefish. Reporters and Secret Service agents in boats about 150 yards away began honking their horns and cheering. It was victory at sea. Paul Bedard, a *Washington Times* reporter, said the news was "like the end of a war."

When the *Fidelity* returned, the mood at the dock was as wild as Election Night. Barbara Bush thrust her fist high in the air in celebration. Relatives shouted for joy. Grandchildren kissed him.

When a reporter asked the President if he was going to have the fish stuffed and mounted, Bush replied, "Stuff it? I'm lucky to have caught it."

Herbert Hoover
The White House, 1929

Long before Watergate the White House was involved in a shocking cover-up—a fishy scandal perpetrated by none other than President Herbert Hoover himself.

The victims of this ignoble intrigue were the directors of a prestigious fishing club who for years had personally brought their first salmon of the season to the White House and presented it to the President. The Chief Executive would dutifully pose with the directors and their fish for photos that were later framed and hung on the walls of the club.

In 1929 the directors arrived at the White House for the annual ritual. Before the formal presentation they gave the prize salmon to President Hoover's new secretary. Unfortunately, he was uninformed and didn't follow the usual procedure of simply keeping the fish on ice until the photo session began. Instead, the secretary gave the fish to the White House chef.

At the start of the photo session Hoover turned to his secretary and asked, "Where's the salmon?" The secretary, with a stricken look on his face, stammered, "I . . . uh . . . sent it to the . . . um . . . kitchen. I thought you . . . uh . . . were going to eat it."

Hoover rolled his eyes and immediately dispatched the flustered secretary to the kitchen. There, to his horror, he found that the salmon's head and tail had been cut off, and its entrails had been cleaned out.

But one of the cooks took immediate action. She rapidly sewed the head and tail back onto the fish and neatly stuffed its insides with cotton. The secretary then rushed the fish out to the White House lawn, where Hoover, the club directors, and the photographers were waiting.

The presidential coverup was now under way. As he handed the stuffed salmon to the President, the secretary whispered a warning to him: "Hold the fish carefully and horizontally."

Hoover triumphantly held the fish up and smiled for the cameras. It looked as if no one would be the wiser. But then one of the photographers stepped up to Hoover and whispered, "Mr. President, something's wrong with the fish." Hoover looked down and was aghast to see cotton sticking out of the salmon. He then hid the offending evidence.

Confessing to the cover-up years later, Hoover said in his memoirs, "A President must be equal to such emergencies, so I carefully held up the fish with my hand over the spot of cotton. The directors of the fishing club, the fish, and I posed before twenty photographers—and each asked for 'just one more' six times. But the cotton kept oozing out of the fish as was proved by later photographs."

Those last photos never made it onto the walls of the fishing club.

The Only Thing They Have to Fear
Is Fear Itself

President Franklin D. Roosevelt loved to fish—even though he wasn't particularly successful at it.

Returning from a trip to one of his favorite rivers, the Brule River in Wisconsin's Northwoods, FDR was asked if he had had any luck.

"Well," replied the President, "I estimate that there are forty-five thousand fish in the River Brule, and although I've caught hardly any of them, I've intimidated them."

Jimmy Carter

Plains, Georgia, 1979

No fishing story received more press or caused so much political damage as the one President Jimmy Carter told. It may have been the killing blow in his bid for reelection.

In early 1979 Carter was fishing from his canoe on his farm pond in Plains, Georgia, when he heard a strange hissing noise like air escaping from a punctured tire. He then spotted a rabbit swimming straight toward him. It wasn't a cutesy, cuddly bunny but rather a big splay-footed swamp rabbit hissing menacingly with its nostrils flared.

The animal was either fleeing from some predator or berserk. Having limited experience with enraged rabbits, Carter didn't know what its motives were. However, he did know that this large, wet, hissing animal was intent on climbing into the presidential canoe.

Carter leapt into action, grabbing a paddle and swatting the oncoming varmint. Until that chilling moment the President had never been one to split hares. But now, with his safety on the line, he had no choice. After thwarting the assault Carter was relieved that he wasn't hurt. Apparently, neither was the rabbit, which swam away.

The President never said a word about the rabbit attack until a few months later. At an informal White House gathering he divulged the incident to some of his aides with whom he had been swapping fishing stories.

Recalled press secretary Jody Powell in his book *The Other Side of the Story:* "Had I been doing my job, I would have stopped the President at that moment, pointed out the dangers to him and his administration if such a story ever got out, and sworn him and all within reach of his voice to secrecy. Sadly, I did nothing of the kind. . . . I thought it was funny. Can you imagine such a thing? Faced with a mortal threat to the Carter presidency, I laughed."

For some inexplicable reason, just before the Democratic Convention, Powell leaked the entire story to Brooks Jackson, an Associated Press White House reporter.

The next day AP reported to the world: "President Carter

beat back an attacking rabbit with a canoe paddle as he fished near his Plains, Ga., home last spring. . . . Carter was not injured, and reports are unclear about what became of the rabbit, dubbed the 'Banzai Bunny.' "

The Washington Post ran the story on the front page with the headline: PRESIDENT ATTACKED BY RABBIT. All three TV networks reported the bunny assault.

Columnists, editorial writers, and comedians had a field day. Conservative George Will called the President's response timid because he shooed the rabbit away rather than having the brute shot by the Secret Service. At the other end of the political spectrum columnist Mary McGrory considered the brandishing of the paddle a clear example of excessive force. Was this the sort of behavior that we should accept from the man whose finger was on the nuclear trigger?

The Boston Globe said that this shocking fishing story could drive memories of Chappaquiddick from the minds of American voters, thus clearing the way for Senator Ted Kennedy to reclaim the family estate on Pennsylvania Avenue.

Then there was the credibility factor. Was Carter telling us the truth? Ed Peifer, national secretary of the American Rabbit Breeders Association, declared, "I've never heard of an attack rabbit . . . though once in a while you do get a mean one."

"It was a nightmare," Powell recalled. "The story ran for more than a week. The President was repeatedly asked to explain his behavior at town hall meetings, press conferences, and meetings with editors."

This one fishing story triggered the beginning of the end for the Carter administration. The whole idea of an attack rabbit was laughable—and Carter, whose popularity was shaky at the time, couldn't afford to have people laughing at him. The image of the President of the United States fending off a "violent" bunny rabbit with a canoe paddle was just a little too much for most voters to take.

When the votes for Ronald Reagan and Jimmy Carter were tallied, the result for Carter was the same as the ending of a Looney Tunes cartoon: "Tha-tha-that's all, folks!"

Richard Nixon

1952

Of all the U.S. Presidents, Richard Nixon was one of the worst . . . at fishing.

Even he admitted it. In his book *In the Arena* Nixon confessed that "fishing just isn't my bag." In fact, he was as dangerous with a fishing rod in his hand as he was with a tape recorder.

"I tried deep-sea fishing once as a teenager and gave it up because I used to get seasick," he said. "When I told Winston Churchill in 1954 of my problem, he said, 'Don't worry, young man, as you get older, you will outgrow it.' I was forty-one years old at the time."

Despite his aversion to fishing Nixon felt compelled to wield a rod and reel shortly after the Republican Convention in 1952, when he was nominated as Dwight Eisenhower's running mate. Ike, who was an ardent fisherman, "encouraged" Nixon to join him on a fishing trip. Nixon could hardly say no to the next President of the United States.

Eisenhower figured that as soon as Nixon was exposed to the great outdoors, he would get hooked on fishing. So Ike took him to a mountain stream and tried to teach him how to fly-cast for trout.

"It was a disaster," Nixon recalled.

Like a father teaching his son to fish Ike patiently explained the intricacies of casting to Nixon. Finally, the novice fisherman was ready for his first cast. He flicked his wrist and let fly—and hooked a tree limb.

Eisenhower smiled grimly and gave his running mate some further tips. Nixon nodded that he understood fully and tossed out another cast—and snagged his line on the same tree branch.

Ike gritted his teeth but refused to let Nixon quit. He told Nixon to try again. At least Nixon was consistent—he hooked the same limb for the third straight time.

Eisenhower took Nixon's fly-casting failures as a personal challenge and was determined to tutor the novice angler until he got it right. Once more Ike gave Nixon some pointers and then ordered him to cast again.

By now Nixon wished he were on the campaign trail, angling for votes instead of learning to cast. Reluctantly, he let loose with another cast—and hooked Eisenhower on the shirt!

That was it for Ike. The man who had helped win World War II, and refused to ever face defeat, now surrendered. "The lesson ended abruptly," Nixon recalled. "I could see that he was disappointed."

Ike never asked Nixon to go fishing again.

THE ONES
THAT
GOT AWAY

The Most Absurd
Ways Anglers
Lost Their Catch

Jim Bitter

James River, Virginia, 1989

Jim Bitter committed the costliest fumble by a pro in fishing-tournament history.

After landing the bass that would have made him the winner of competitive bass fishing's biggest event, Bitter accidentally dropped it over the side—and wound up losing the tournament by a mere two ounces.

The Florida fishing guide's goof cost him not only prestige, but also the fifty-thousand-dollar first-place prize in the 1989 B.A.S.S. Masters Classic.

The experience was literally a Bitter disappointment.

After seeing the fish, then the title and the money slip from his grasp, he broke down in tears of frustration. "That was certainly the most expensive fish I ever lost—and definitely the most embarrassing," Bitter moaned.

It was a nightmare ending to what had begun as a fairy tale come true. The little-heralded fisherman had been thrilled earlier in the year when he won the 1989 Megabucks Tourney. In August he entered the Classic—his first—with high hopes of snagging the important title.

For the first two days Bitter was the undisputed leader and threatened to run away with the event, which was held on the James River near Richmond, Virginia. Entering the third and final day of the tourney, Bitter held a hefty five-pound lead. Since the James River isn't known as a big bass haven, those five pounds seemed insurmountable.

It looked as if the other fishermen didn't have a chance when Bitter reeled in three bass before nine-thirty A.M.—and all were keepers over twelve inches in length.

Confident of victory, Bitter relaxed and joked around with TV camera crews who were stationed in nearby boats recording the tourney leader's every move.

Around noon, while fishing close to shore, he tangled with the biggest fish of the tournament—a largemouth that appeared to weigh more than seven pounds. But the stubborn bass leapt into the air, cleared a tree limb, and snapped the line.

Bitter gazed at the fish's splashdown spot with a tortured look on his face. "That fish would have ended any doubt about this tournament," he said wistfully. His only comforts were his sizable lead and the fact that more than three hours of fishing still remained. But for the next two hours he never caught so much as an old boot.

"I was certain that if I caught one more keeper, I would win the Classic and the fifty-thousand-dollar prize," Bitter said. With less than an hour to go he caught that fish. But it wasn't a big fish, and he decided he'd better measure it before he put it into the live well to make certain it was the fish he needed to win. Bitter put his measuring board on top of the console and measured the bass. It was thirteen inches long—an inch over the minimum limit.

"I was elated because I knew I had it won," said Bitter. "Then I picked the fish back up to put him into the live well and he just sort of squirted out of my hands.

"The fish hit the windshield and glanced off it like a rocket. I lunged for him, but I never even got close. He bounced right back into the water. Just like that it was over."

Ol' Bitterfingers didn't catch another fish the rest of the afternoon. When he got back to the dock, his day's catch totaled six pounds seven ounces, giving him a three-day total of thirty-one pounds four ounces.

But to his horror another fisherman, Hank Parker, of TV fame—who'd started the morning in eighth place—had enjoyed a great day fishing. Parker's three-day catch totalled thirty-one pounds six ounces . . . two teensy-weensy ounces more than Bitter's!

At the awards ceremony Parker took a victory lap around Richmond Coliseum in a towed boat and trailer as fifteen thousand fishing fans roared their approval. Meanwhile, Bitter hid his face and fought to keep his emotions under control.

"Losing the fish was bad enough," he said later. "But as it turned out, when I lost the fish, there was a boat close by with a camera crew from the local TV station, and they filmed the whole thing. I got to see it that night on the local news. And again . . . and again . . . and again. . . .

"I've never done anything that stupid in my life."

There was a certain irony in this fumble that didn't go unnoticed by the former researcher for the Florida Game and Fresh Water Fish Commission. "I figured it up," Bitter said. "In my twelve years with the commission I handled about twenty thousand fish and I never lost a one over the side. Nice timing, huh?"

A. Ray Cockrell

Destin, Florida, 1988

A. Ray Cockrell wasn't just an unsuspecting angler who ate his fish only to find out later that it would have been a world record; he was an unsuspecting angler who ate a fish and gave two others away only to find out later that they *all* would have been world records. As if that weren't exasperating enough, he unwittingly let three other potential record-holders go free!

"I was always astounded whenever I heard stories that someone ate a world-record fish," Cockrell said. "I didn't see how it could happen. Now I know firsthand."

Cockrell, of Loganville, Georgia, was temporarily living in Destin, Florida, while working on a condominium project. "I was bored to death on weekends," he explained, "so I did a little surf fishing just to pass the time."

On June 3, 1988, Cockrell began fishing in the surf off Destin, using cut bonito for bait. It turned into an extraordinary day as one gigantic bluefish after another struck his line.

When he hauled in the first blue, he didn't even know what kind of fish it was. He laid it on the beach, where people soon gathered around, oohing and ahhing. Cockrell felt proud about the catch but had no inkling it might be a world record. In less than an hour he landed six bruisers, from about thirty-two to forty-two pounds. Any one of them would have been a world record, according to Captain Joy Dunlap, a representative of the International Game Fish Association, who later investigated the catch.

Cockrell, who took pictures of the fish, let three of them go. He gave two others away and kept the largest, which he weighed at a local bait-and-tackle store. The fish tipped the scales at a whopping forty-two pounds—more than ten pounds over the world all-tackle record. Unfortunately, no one at the bait shop told Cockrell that his fish might be a record.

"And I didn't think to check," he lamented. "I took it home, cleaned it, cooked it, and ate it instead."

So when an IGFA representative visited Cockrell and told him what the world record was, it was too late. "Cockrell was using a thirty-pound line and any one of his fish would have broken the current all-tackle record of thirty-one pounds twelve ounces," said Captain Dunlap. "He lost two records— the thirty-pound record and the all tackle."

How could a fisherman ignore six potential world-record fish? "I just wasn't thinking," admitted Cockrell.

Ironically, Cockrell says he's an outstanding fisherman who fishes nearly every day . . . but for bass. "I could tell you off the top of my head the exact weight of the world-record bass and who caught it," he said. "But I just don't know enough about saltwater fish. In fact, until Destin, I hadn't been saltwater fishing in more than ten years, and then it was in California.

"I plan on doing more surf fishing. And from now on I'll make sure to check the records first before I eat another big fish."

Norman Strung

A Minnesota Lake, 1969

Fishermen are always lamenting over the big one that got away. But more than once veteran outdoor writer Norman Strung has wished the big one had gotten away. It would have saved him from much embarrassment.

One time, in 1969, Strung was fishing for pike on a Minnesota lake, where he met two fellow anglers. When Strung introduced himself to the pair, they recognized his name from bylines in leading outdoor publications.

"They immediately elevated me to expert-fisherman status, something I find both unwarranted and uncomfortable," he recalled. "As a 'star' I was asked all manner of questions about pike and pike fishing that I tried to answer to the best of my limited knowledge."

The next morning the three men went fishing together and Strung managed to land a ten-pound northern pike early, further confirming, in the eyes of his new friends, his status as an "expert."

Then it happened.

"Around midmorning I got a tremendous strike," he said. "The rod was nearly yanked out of my hand. I set the hook but the line snapped almost immediately. 'I've caught a lot of pike,' I told my fishing companions, 'but I've never had anything hit like that. It had to be a monster. I'd give anything just to have a look at something that big.'

"As lousy luck would have it, my wish was granted two minutes later when one of my companions noticed a small surface disturbance behind the boat. It appeared to be a fish in its death throes."

Motoring back to the fish, they found a skinny two-pound northern—the kind known locally as a "hammer handle" because it's so small and thin. Strung didn't even give it a second look—until he noticed that his lure was still in its mouth. That little two-pounder was his monster fish!

"I wished that I had never said I had hooked a monster," Strung recalled. "Then I began mumbling something to my companions about inertia, kinetic energy, and how the fish

17

must have hit on the run. At least nobody asked me any more questions about pike fishing after that."

Another time Strung was trolling for snapper in Mexico when he had a tremendous strike. The twenty-pound test line he was using nearly flew off the reel.

"I couldn't control it," Strung recalled. "Line zipped off the spool and I told my guide that it felt as though I had hooked a trailer truck." But the fish had become entangled in a snag and couldn't be budged.

Strung cursed his bad luck. He hated the thought of losing his expensive lure, not to mention the huge fish below. But then his Mexican guide volunteered to jump overboard and rescue the snagged lure. When he emerged from the murky water, the guide triumphantly held up the line and the lure and the "huge" snapper.

"Here is the big one that got away, señor," the guide said with a wide grin. It was nothing more than a three-pound snapper! Certainly not a fish of "trailer truck" proportions.

The most shameful "big one" that Strung wished had gotten away but didn't was dredged up from the headwaters of the Missouri River in 1975. He was in a rowboat with his wife, casting a lure to likely-looking spots as they drifted down the river.

Wham! A strike, a big strike. Strung felt his adversary roll from side to side—just as a big trout would do when it first feels the hook. Strung yelled for his wife to take the oars while he moved to the front of the boat to better fight the huge fish.

"Each time it shook its head or twisted its body, the drag would relent," Strung said. "I could not gain on the fish. I had to get to shore." After his wife rowed him to the riverbank, Strung clambered out of the boat and continued the fight.

"I ran down the bank, following the fish," he recalled. "By careful pressure born of long years of experience, I managed to lead the now tiring fish out of the swift water into a calm backwater. The battle was nearly won. Net in hand, I peered down into the water as the fish neared my rod tip. I had to be careful. A last mighty lunge could still break the light line and I'd lose what surely was a trophy.

"Then I saw it. It was large and round and smooth . . . it was a rock! I had caught a rock! It was like a cannonball, with just one tiny, deep hole in it and that's where my hook had lodged." Strung had fought an epic battle with a rock, not recognizing the difference between the rock's movement in the current and a fish's. But Strung still got his trophy.

"That rock weighed fifteen pounds three ounces," he said. "I mounted it on a board, and it now hangs in my office."

Fred Holland
Arthur Smith King Mackerel Tournament, 1986

Fred Holland let more than a giant fish slip through his fingers—he let sixty thousand dollars slip away too. His "one that got away" was a shameful heartbreaker.

Holland was one of 6,212 ardent anglers in 1,244 boats competing in the largest and richest fishing contest in the world—the Arthur Smith King Mackerel Tournament. It was held along a seventy-mile stretch of the South Carolina coast in 1986. At stake were $540,000 in prizes, including $60,000 for the biggest kingfish.

During the tourney Holland, of Carolina Beach, North Carolina, landed a huge king that weighed about fifty pounds. It looked like a sure winner.

As he pulled his boat up to the dock by the weigh station, Holland saw a crowd of photographers who clamored for him to show off his fish. The proud angler enthusiastically lifted the fish up over his head for the cameras. But to his horror the prize king slipped from his hands, hit the dock, and splashed into the water.

It sank like a stone.

Everyone gazed into the dark, turbid Intracoastal Waterway, but there was no sign of the fish.

"Don't give up hope," said Arthur Smith, the entertainer and Charlotte sportsman for whom the tournament is named. "Dead fish usually float, don't they?"

Sadly, Holland's didn't.

Holland frantically strode up and down the dock, looking for some sign of the fish. In desperation he even hired two scuba divers to search for it. No dice. The divers couldn't find the king either.

Holland's fish got away—and so did all that first-place prize money. "He did everything but cry," Smith said. There was one small consolation. Holland received five hundred dollars as the recipient of the Goody's Headache Powder Award—which went to the angler with the toughest luck of the tournament.

Bernie Schultz
Rodman Reservoir, Florida, 1980

Most fishermen, sooner or later, know what it's like to "let the big one get away." But pro bass angler Bernie Schultz found a new way to lose one—after it was already in the live well.

Schultz, a member of the Fenwick East Coast Fishing Team and a B.A.S.S. Masters Classic competitor, suffered his moment of shame shortly before he started his tournament career.

"I was relatively inexperienced with high-performance boats back then," he recalled. "But I had just gotten a brand-new Hydra-Sport bass boat with a hundred-fifteen-horse-power engine. It wasn't even three days old. I just couldn't wait to take it out and show it off, so I called three friends to go fishing."

One of his buddies brought his own boat, so they split up with two in each boat and launched their crafts at the famous Rodman Reservoir near Ocala, Florida. Schultz knew that he would have to drive the boat cautiously, because the Rodman is a winding, twisting lake with a lot of standing timber. It can be mighty unforgiving to a careless boater.

After fishing together for nearly an hour without a strike, his friends decided to try another spot. But Schultz didn't want to leave the area. So his partner jumped in the other boat and the three of them went down to another part of the lake.

"Not long after they left, I got the big one—a beautiful eight-pound largemouth bass," Schultz recalled. "Well, I couldn't wait to show them. I put the bass in the live well and fired up the engine and took off to find them.

"I was running pretty fast through the old river channel when I came to this really tight turn, probably a hundred-twenty-degree bend. I was still inexperienced with the boat and I took the turn too fast. As soon as I got into it, I realized I was going to slide the boat into the trees lining the bend. I panicked. I cut the throttle hard, and when I did, the bow plunged down into the water, and the boat rolled right over. It was weird. There I was in the driver's seat—upside down seeing things from under the water."

Schultz watched helplessly as his tackle began falling slowly to the bottom, while the rest of his prized gear fluttered down after it.

Then he saw his live-well door swing open and out swam his eight-pound trophy, freed from a deadly fate by the mishap. *Oh, no, not that,* Schultz said to himself. *Who's going to believe me now?*

Had he stayed under water much longer, Schultz would have lost more than just a bass and his gear. "I finally got out of the seat before I drowned and I swam up for a gulp of air," Schultz recalled. "Then I climbed onto the overturned hull and started screaming for help. I guess I must have looked pretty comical sitting on top of my overturned boat hollering. When my friends heard me and came over, they broke up laughing as soon as they saw me."

They managed to get the boat rolled back over and then towed it back to the ramp. "That's the most embarrassed I've ever been," said Schultz. "My one-that-got-away story wasn't only about that bass. It was about my boat too."

Chris Christian
Chattanooga, Tennessee, 1986

Florida outdoor writer Chris Christian often dreamed of catching the "big one." But when his dream finally came true, it turned into a nightmare . . . in front of fifteen thousand people.

Besides having spent years as a bass guide on the St. Johns River, Christian was the outdoor editor of the *Palatka Daily News* in Florida, senior writer for *Southern Outdoors* magazine, and an editor for *Florida Sportsman* magazine.

In 1986 he was invited to fish the Bassmaster Classic in Chattanooga, Tennessee, as a press observer. The Classic has always been the Super Bowl of bass fishing. Weigh-ins are held in large auditoriums with thousands of spectators, TV cameras, and at least several hundred outdoor writers. Each pro bass fisherman earns a spot in the Classic based on how many points he's piled up in other tournaments throughout the year. During the tourney each angler is paired with an invited press observer.

As each day ends, the fisherman and his boat are wheeled into the auditorium. There he weighs in his catch as master of ceremonies and B.A.S.S. president Ray Scott introduces him to the crowd.

It's quite a spectacle.

The 1986 tournament featured a special competition for the outdoor writers. Each writer could keep one bass, and the largest bass caught by a writer would win five hundred dollars each for the writer and his pro partner.

Christian was paired with defending champion Jack Chancellor on the final day. Chancellor was having an uncharacteristically bad tournament. He was so far down on the leader board, he needed binoculars to see whose name was on top. He knew that his best shot at earning any money was the five hundred dollars he could win if Christian bagged the biggest bass among the writers. So Chancellor told Christian to go ahead and fish as hard as he could and not worry about getting in his way. Normally, the pro takes the more advantageous front of the boat and works the best spots, while the writer takes what's left.

Christian fished from the bow and came up with a big bass—a four-and-a-half-pounder, which was virtually a sure winner in the writer's pool. As they got into the weigh-in line that afternoon, a quick check of the leader board showed that Christian's fish would win easily.

"I knew that Ray Scott would have me up on the weigh-in stand for a quick interview in front of the cameras," recalled Christian. "So I got my clothes all straightened out, combed my hair, and got ready for my big moment in front of fifteen thousand people.

"Our turn came and they handed me a fish bag. I slipped the fish out of the live well and into the bag, trying to be very cool and casual about it. When Ray saw the size of the fish, he told me to hold it up for the crowd. So, standing on our bass boat, I reached in and held it up. The crowd oohed and ahhed and applauded."

Then the fish gave a convulsive twist and Christian dropped it. The bass almost fell into Chancellor's lap, but the angler leapt out of the way as it landed in the boat seat. Christian made a desperate grab for it and sprawled over the seat— while the fish flopped onto the deck.

"First, someone snickered . . . then laughter started breaking out," he recalled. "I got down on my hands and knees and tried to grab that fish again—and it still slithered away. Finally I just belly-flopped on it and got it back into the bag. But by then the crowd was roaring.

"I managed to make my way up to the weigh-in stand without further stumbling. But I was mortified. I had never really been laughed at before, certainly not by fifteen thousand people. I did win the writer's prize and that five-hundred-dollar check was nice. But I'm not sure I'd go through that again for twice the money."

Benny Ray Long

Clinch River, Virginia, 1965

Benny Ray Long was one of the most respected fishermen in Coeburn, Virginia, until he rushed into town one day with an incredibly wild tale about the one that got away.

Long claimed he saw a worm catch a fish! But after a furious struggle the fish swam off.

Ever since he first told that story—which to this day he swears is true—his fishing reputation has been mud.

Nobody, not even his minister, believed his wacky account and he was roundly shamed for telling a whopper.

"I've had to live with being called a liar ever since that day twenty-five years ago," said Long, a deeply religious carpet installer. "But I wasn't lying then, and I ain't lying now.

"It happened around 1965. I went fishing all the time back then, and I could catch dozens of fish when everybody around me wasn't even getting a bite.

"One day I went looking for some different kind of bait. Down in a creek that flows into the Clinch River, I found some grampuses—big black things that live in the water and that we always called worms. They're tough as leather and have a pair of pincers on one end, like sharp lobster claws.

"Well, one of those grampuses was the biggest I'd ever seen. He was about four inches long with a thick body, and his pincers were real wicked looking. And he was mean. Real mean.

"I took him down to the river and baited him on a big hook. That ornery old cuss squirmed like crazy and was trying to get at me with those pincers all the while. I finally got him on the hook and cast my line about fifteen feet out from shore. I sat down and waited. Pretty soon I felt a tug on my line and gave a yank.

"The next thing I saw was the dangedest sight anybody could imagine. A small bass about a foot long suddenly came shooting up out of the water—with my grampus clamped tight onto his upper lip. The fish wasn't hooked at all, except by the grampus's pincers.

"That fish was just dancing through the air, slapping from side to side trying to work itself loose from the grampus's pincers. But that old worm just held on.

"The bass splashed down again and both of them disappeared under the water. Then the water started boiling as that fish and worm fought it out underwater.

"A few seconds later the bass popped into the air again—and this time the grampus was clamped onto his back! I'll never know how that worm managed to move from one spot to the other on the fish without it getting away, but he did. He was determined to land that fish, I reckon.

"I started working the fish toward shore. But just as I got him up close and started to grab him, he gave a mighty fling and broke loose from the grampus's pincers. I guess the worm was getting tired by then. The bass splashed back into the river.

"Believe it or not, that fish looked relieved as he swam away. And the grampus looked as disappointed as I was."

When Long told his story to his fishing buddies in town, they just snorted in derision. Recalled Long, "They said things like 'You've been out in the sun too long' and 'Man, you must think we're stupid to believe that.'

"I even tried to get my preacher to believe me the next Sunday, but he just looked at me like I was the biggest liar God ever made, and then he walked away shaking his head.

"After all these years I still haven't found a soul who'll believe me. Now I'm an old man and I reckon I'll go to my grave branded as the man who made up the biggest fish story in Wise County, Virginia.

"But every word of it is absolutely true."

FISHING TRIP-UPS

**The Craziest
Things
That Happened
on a
Fishing Trip**

John Jenkins
North Kent Coast, England, 1981

The British are known for their calm determination in the face of disaster. John Jenkins certainly faced incredible disaster calmly . . . but not necessarily intelligently.

Jenkins's moment of ignobility began on a sunny Thursday in August 1981, when the prosperous farmer decided to take his family fishing. They piled into a four-wheel-drive Dodge truck and headed for some nearby mud flats close to the resort area of Seasalter. About a mile out on the flats their truck got stuck.

Although it was upsetting, it was hardly a disaster. Jenkins made the long trek back to the road, found a telephone, and had a farmhand bring one of his tractors to the rescue. The tractor made it out to the truck—and, unfortunately, got stuck too.

Still, it wasn't a disaster.

The family climbed out of the truck and everyone headed back to the road, but not before they watched the incoming tide do what it does best—come in. The tide covered their truck and their tractor.

Now it was fast approaching a disaster. But the worst was yet to come. The next morning Jenkins arrived back at the scene on a second tractor that he owned and quickly pulled the first tractor out of the mud. He and his farmhand then drove the two tractors toward the Dodge. But they got stuck too. Now Jenkins had three vehicles mired on the mud flats— but he was still undaunted. He owned one more tractor, so he returned and brought it to the rescue.

Yes . . . it, too, got stuck. Jenkins now had four vehicles —three tractors and a truck—stuck on the mud flats. And once again the tide rolled in. Before long all four of his vehicles disappeared beneath the mighty tides of the North Kent coast. Most anyone would have considered this ordeal a complete disaster and would have given up. But not Jenkins. He was no quitter. He had another plan.

By Saturday morning word of Jenkins's misfortunes had spread and whole families traveled out to the mud flats to watch the drama. This time Jenkins was back with a mechanical digger and he diligently went to work and rescued one tractor and returned it safely to land. That was the good news. The bad news was that the mechanical digger then got stuck. Without it Jenkins couldn't rescue any more of his vehicles. By Saturday night the digger was underwater with his three other vehicles.

Through it all Jenkins kept his stiff upper British lip and did not outwardly scream or cry, not that anyone would have blamed him if he had.

On Sunday morning Jenkins was back on the mud flats again with his newly rescued tractor for still another attempt. But, not surprisingly, it quickly became mired in the mud, joining the mechanical digger, the Dodge truck, and the other two tractors. Then the tide rolled in again and covered Jenkins's entire farm fleet, which were lost for good.

Disaster.

Fred Barbeau
A Minnesota Lake, 1972

To Bill Cork, good buddy Fred Barbeau is a terrific rain-maker. That's great if you're in the middle of a drought. But it's lousy if you're on a lake trying to fish.

Bill, public-relations manager at Plano Tackle Box, and Fred have been best friends for many years. Both love to fish, and they often went out on the water together.

But after ten outings over a two-year span, Bill absolutely refused to fish with Fred anymore.

The reason was simple yet strange—Bill just got tired of getting wet. That's because no matter what was forecast for the weather, no matter what the time of year or the condition of the sky, when Fred went fishing with Bill, it rained. Every time.

"He draws rain like a magnet," Bill explained. "People will think I'm exaggerating, but believe me, I'm not. There has never been a time Fred went fishing with me that it didn't rain. It can be a beautiful day, but as soon as Fred puts his line in the water, the sky opens up. I've often told him he should move to Ethiopia to help end the drought there."

Added Fred, "I can't explain it. When I'm with Bill, it rains. To save our friendship we finally stopped going fishing together."

Bill felt compelled to exile Fred from any future fishing plans. Years went by, and although Bill and Fred remained friends, they didn't fish together. Finally, Bill—feeling guilty over entertaining so foolish an idea as a jinx—decided that maybe all this rain stuff with Fred was just one weird coincidence.

"I figured I'd take him fishing under conditions that made rain absolutely impossible," Bill recalled. "I had the perfect place in mind—ice fishing in the middle of February . . . in Minnesota. There was absolutely no way Fred could jinx that outing."

Fred had mixed emotions. He was delighted that Bill had invited him to go on the trip, since Fred had never been ice fishing before. On the other hand, "I warned Bill of my 'ability' to attract rain." But Bill figured they wouldn't have to worry about Fred causing it to rain, because it was the dead of winter. So, full of optimism, the two anglers left on a Friday after work and drove four hundred miles to a beautiful frozen lake.

The night was frigid, with temperatures below zero. There were eighteen inches of snow on the ground and three feet of ice on the lake. There was absolutely no talk—not even a thought—of rain. Bill and Fred got a good night's sleep in a motel and the next morning they headed for a local bait shop.

As they stepped outside, it seemed surprisingly warm to Bill. He gazed up at the sky, but it looked innocent enough. After all, it was February, it had been below zero the night before, and they were in Minnesota . . . naaah . . . it couldn't rain . . . could it?

Loaded with minnows, wax worms, and tips from the bait shop on where to fish, the pair drove four miles to the lake. Quickly unloading their ice-fishing gear, they headed for the spot they were told would produce nice jumbo perch.

"It was really a beautiful morning," said Bill. "We set up our gear and started drilling holes. We no sooner had the first hole drilled than it started to drizzle. I couldn't believe it. A warm front had moved in and the drizzle became harder and harder. Within an hour it was raining steadily.

"I looked at Fred and he looked at me and said, 'I told you, I told you. I can make it rain anywhere.' We both just started laughing. Then we packed up and headed home.

"We're still good friends. But I haven't gone fishing with him since."

Bill Cork
Mississippi River, Thomson, Illinois, 1985

It was a fishing weekend in hell.

Everything went wrong that could go wrong for Bill Cork and his two buddies after they planned to fish the backwaters of the Mississippi near Thomson, Illinois, and camp out for two nights.

"If you hang around this sport long enough, you're bound to have a trip like this one," said Cork.

The trio borrowed a fourteen-foot flat-bottom johnboat and strapped it onto the roof of Cork's station wagon. To make sure it didn't fall off, the men wound yards of rope around the boat. Once it was securely lashed down, they loaded in the tent, pots, pans, food, and fishing gear and took off on the two-hour drive from Sandwich, Illinois, to Thomson.

The first hint that the trip was doomed came a few minutes after they'd started—when the boat fell off the car. Fortunately, it wasn't damaged. So Cork and his buddies halted traffic while they picked up the boat, put it back on the car roof, and really roped it down. Twenty miles later it fell off again. They retrieved it and lashed it down even tighter. Forty miles later the boat slid off the roof again. It fell off a *fourth* time after another fifteen miles. If this was an omen, it didn't faze the trio.

When they finally got to Thomson and unloaded their gear, Cork and his pals discovered they had forgotten to bring one important item—the motor. So they drove into the nearest town and tried to rent one. No such luck. "We went back to the river and decided to row," recalled Cork. "We were strong, we were healthy, we had oars, and we figured we could do it the old-fashioned way."

By then it was dark, so they stuck some poles on the bank and set out lines. A short while later, while they were eating burnt home-fries and undercooked burgers, they heard the ringing of a bell that was tied to one of the poles on the bank. Cork raced down to the water's edge to see what fish had been caught. Instead he discovered what the fish had caught. It had pulled the rod and reel into the river and disappeared.

Beginning to wonder if their trip was jinxed, the three men retired to their tent for the night and waited for the next bad thing to happen. They didn't have long to wait. A few hours into the night a storm blew through, knocking their tent over and soaking the trio. They spent the remainder of the night huddled in Cork's station wagon.

The next morning dawned bright and clear and the guys figured the worst was over. After resetting the tent they hung their sleeping bags out to dry, bailed four feet of water out of the boat, and set off for a day of fishing. They had been warned that the river was full of submerged tree stumps, but they didn't see any—until they got stranded on top of one. They managed to get unsnagged only to get stuck on other stumps. Time and again they had to jump overboard in waist-deep water to wrestle the boat free.

Needless to say, they didn't catch a fish all day.

Finally, sick of the stumps and the lack of fish, they rowed back to camp for a nice hot supper. That's when they noticed that the package of powdered potatoes they had brought along wasn't powdered potatoes. It was oatmeal. Somehow the combination of hamburgers and oatmeal didn't sound too appealing. Disgusted, Cork grabbed a beer and plopped down in a lawn chair to ponder what to do next. The lawn chair collapsed.

"We all laughed as I untangled myself from the wreckage of the lawn chair," Cork recalled. "But that was the final straw. We packed up and headed home—one day early."

Wallace Lewis
Spring River, Missouri, 1922

Wallace Lewis was a bass-fishing fanatic who fancied himself an expert angler. He was a neatness freak, from his tackle box to his fishing clothes. He never seemed to get dirty or wet or even sweaty. If it weren't for the fine catches he always brought home, no one who saw him would have believed he fished.

But at least for one day his reputation as the perfectly neat angler was all bull.

Fishing from the bank along a river that sliced through a friend's farm, Lewis hooked the biggest bass he had ever seen. "He cut all the capers he knew, but he was well-hooked," Lewis recalled. "I was enjoying the fight of my life when there was a deafening bellow."

Lewis, annoyed at the distraction at such a critical yet

cherished moment, turned around and gasped. A few hundred yards away was an enraged bull that apparently didn't take kindly to any fisherman invading his territory.

"Now, when a bull bellows in rage and is right behind you, there is only one course of action," said Lewis. "And it must be instantaneous or it's too late for action—get out of there as fast as you can."

Lewis desperately looked for a tree to climb, but the nearest one was about a half mile in the distance. There was a fence three hundred yards away, but he knew he couldn't outrun the bull, even with a head start.

Without looking around any further Lewis ignored his catch of a lifetime, flung his rod aside, and scampered to the edge of the bank and leapt spread eagled into the cold, deep water. When he surfaced, he frantically looked for the onrushing bull.

"Imagine my chagrin, not to say anger, to see the bull charging with head and tail up a half mile down the shore, where he did a magnificent job of scattering a picnic party," said Lewis. "He had not even seen me at all. But how was I to know it then?

"The bellow I had heard was one of many general warnings meant for the picnic party, but it cost me the daddy of all bass. The tackle could easily be replaced; the kidding was easy to stand. But, oh, how it hurt to lose that bass!"

George Foti

Florida Keys, 1977

It's one thing to lose a fish. But losing your fishing partner is a whole other matter. And a shameful one at that.

Two well-known south Florida anglers, George Foti and Al Pfleuger, were coming back from a weekend fishing trip in the Florida Keys.

After captaining the boat all weekend, Pfleuger was exhausted and asked Foti to handle the 120-mile drive home while Pfleuger snoozed in the backseat.

Midway through the three-hour drive to Miami from Key West, Foti pulled into a gas station, got out of the car, and went inside. About that time Pfleuger woke up and, hearing the call of nature, left the car and went to the rest room.

Meanwhile, out came Foti. He jumped in the car and took off, thinking Pfleuger was still asleep in the backseat.

About sixty miles later Foti pulled into Pfleuger's driveway and looked back to wake up his partner. To his shock he discovered that Pfleuger wasn't there. Just then Pfleuger's wife came rushing out to tell Foti that he had left his buddy behind. She also delivered a few other messages from her unhappy husband, who had called home when he realized he had been stranded. Foti then high-tailed it back down the highway to retrieve his irked pal.

At least Foti had delivered Pfleuger's car and boat safely . . . two out of three ain't bad.

Joe Bonadona

Río Colorado, Costa Rica, 1973

Nothing could keep Joe Bonadona from his love of fishing for tarpon in Costa Rica—nothing, that is, except ceiling fans and berserk fish.

Joe, a well-known expert angler from Chicago, looked forward all year to his annual trip to the famous Río Colorado Lodge, a jungle fish camp on Costa Rica's east coast. There he plied the tropical rivers for mammoth, feisty tarpon.

In the winter of 1973 Joe spent all his free time making his own customized fiberglass fishing rods to take with him on his dream fishing trip. Night after night he painstakingly handcrafted each rod to his own specifications. By the time he was ready to fly to Central America, Joe had made a dozen rods. Each one was a mini-masterpiece worth at least a hundred dollars, not that he ever considered selling any of them.

When the big day arrived, Joe and his fellow anglers flew to Río Colorado, where the guides hustled the fishermen to the lodge and checked over their gear. Joe carefully unpacked his brand-new customized rods, matched reels to each one, and proudly showed off his impressive work to the guides.

Joe and the other new arrivals decided to grab a quick bite of lunch and then fish the river until dark. So he picked up his tackle and headed for the main lodge. All the fishermen left their rods outside the lodge. But not Joe. He was so proud of his handiwork that he brought ten of his rods with him to the dining room.

Joe couldn't wait to show all the diners what a wonderful job he had done in making those rods. Carrying the poles vertically in both fists, Joe glanced at the patrons and took notice of their signs of admiration. Unfortunately, Joe failed to take notice of the dining room's powerful overhead ceiling fans whirring at full speed.

Seconds after Joe stepped into the room, he felt his rods vibrate and he heard a sickening and loud thwack, thwack, thwack. The blades of a fan had sliced off the tips of his cherished rods! The horror-stricken angler stood frozen in shock

as he helplessly watched the rod tips fall to the hardwood floor.

No one dared laugh. Not after they saw the tears well up in Joe's eyes. When Joe solemnly surveyed the damage, he discovered that all of his new rods had been shorn.

That wasn't the only disaster that befell Joe on a Río Colorado trip. A few years later he was one of three fishermen eagerly casting at rolling tarpon from a small skiff. Joe was in the middle when a one hundred-pound tarpon suddenly leapt into the air—and aimed at the boat. The wild fish flew toward the angler in the front of the skiff, but the fisherman alertly ducked and the airborne tarpon went sailing over his head.

Unfortunately, Joe was looking in another direction and didn't realize that he was about to experience a painful surprise. Because it all happened so fast, there was no time for his companion in the bow to even shout a warning. The huge tarpon slammed into Joe, knocked him down, beat on him twice with its tail, and then flipped out of the boat. Joe lay in a heap—with three broken ribs, a broken foot, and a bruised shoulder.

After that episode Joe didn't look forward to his annual excursion to Río Colorado with the same enthusiasm as he had before. And no one could blame him.

Larry Madison and Ernie St. Clair
Neversink River, New York, 1940

There was a reason why on a Monday afternoon in early May in 1940, New Yorkers found several large brown trout on the corner of Broadway and Forty-second Street.

The trout marked the end of a mortifying fishing trip for Larry Madison and Ernie St. Clair.

According to famed outdoor writer Ed Zern, the two Big

Apple anglers and their friend Jim Deren, owner of New York's famous fly fishing shop, Angler's Roost, drove up on a Sunday to the Catskills for a day's fishing on the Neversink River. After a couple of hours without a bite Jim suggested trying another spot about ten miles away. But Larry and Ernie decided to stay put. So Jim drove off by himself after telling his buddies he'd pick them up at a nearby bridge at dusk.

By the afternoon Larry and Ernie were rewarded for their patience. They each stuffed about a half-dozen good-sized brown trout in their creels and headed to the bridge to wait for their ride with Jim. They waited and waited.

Night fell, yet Jim still hadn't shown. The spring air had turned cold, and they were feeling miserable because their waders had leaked enough to soak their underclothing. Larry and Ernie decided to do a little night fishing in the rushing water under the bridge, hoping the exercise would keep their blood circulating until Jim arrived.

After an hour Jim was still a no-show and they were still cold. They trudged out of the water and built a small fire under the bridge and huddled around it, all the while cursing their missing friend.

By midnight it became apparent that Jim was not coming. It was also apparent that they were in a hell of a mess. They were cold, wet, and hungry and abandoned near a remote road that hadn't seen a vehicle since early afternoon. And the nearest village was eight miles away on the other side of a mountain.

So Larry and Ernie packed up their gear and hiked to the town, which they reached about five A.M. They were footsore, famished, and had a total of fifteen cents between them, since their wallets were in Jim's car. They listened to each other's teeth chatter while waiting for the sleeping burg to awake. Eventually, Larry and Ernie flagged down a New York City–bound bus. After begging and pleading they persuaded the driver to take them aboard.

It was high noon when the weary anglers arrived at the Port Authority Bus Terminal near Times Square. Still clad in their waders, fishing jackets, and fly-bedecked hats, Larry and Ernie clutched their rods and reels and lugged their smelly, bulging creels down the sidewalk.

Even by New York standards the pair looked totally out of place. Their mood wasn't made any better when the hobnails on their fishing boots clattered embarrassingly on the concrete sidewalk and their landing nets kept snagging on people's buttons.

The fishermen's mortification was capped when they reached Broadway and Forty-second Street. That's where the bottom of Larry's creel fell out and spilled sixteen-inch brown trout up and down the sidewalk. Larry was too tired to do anything about it. He just left them there.

The dog-tired duo finally made it to Jim's midtown store, where they hoped to find the answer to where the hell he had been. They hoped Jim hadn't been killed. On the other hand, if he was okay, they were going to kill him.

When they walked into his store, there was Jim. He took one look at the tuckered-out, ripe anglers and burst out laughing. Before they had a chance to strangle him, Jim explained what had happened.

As he was driving back to the bridge to pick them up, his car had a flat tire. He arrived late and had been unable to find them in the darkness. He honked his horn and hollered for them for almost an hour. Apparently, the roar of the fast water beneath the bridge had drowned out Jim's honking and shouting. Then he figured that they had gone back to the city with an angler whom the trio had met on the river earlier that morning. So he left.

"Sorry I laughed at you guys when you came in," Jim told them. "But you're quite a sight."

Larry glowered. "You wouldn't look any better if you had fished all day, then froze in cold, wet clothes while huddling under a bridge through most of the night, walked eight miles over a mountain, begged a ride on a bus, and not had any food or sleep in thirty some hours."

"Yeah, I guess you're right," said Jim. "I'm sorry. By the way, where are your fish?"

"Forty-second and Broadway," replied Larry, "and don't ask why."

BRAIN SPRAINS

The Most Mind-Boggling Mental Miscues

Burma Thomas
Guntersville Lake, Alabama, 1979

By 1990 Burma Thomas had won fourteen national fishing titles, including two Bass'n Gal Classics, and placed in the money dozens of times. But she will always be short one money-winning finish—simply because she couldn't count.

"It was back in the days when I was just starting out in professional fishing," Burma recalled. "I didn't even know they had a circuit for women, so I fished any tournament I could get in. I was accepted in a Red Man Tournament on Guntersville Lake in Alabama, and I was the only woman in the tournament. My partner and I had a great day. We caught lots of bass and started culling our catch early."

Each fisherman was allowed to enter seven fish in the tournament. So when the anglers reached their limit, they began to release the smallest bass in the live well each time they caught one bigger—a practice called "culling."

Because Burma's boat had only one live well, she and her partner each made a separate mark on each of their fish so they could tell which fish was theirs. By the end of the day both anglers had culled six bass each.

Burma was elated with her success and felt confident that she would win some decent money. When she got back to the dock, she started to dig her fish out of the live well and count them. Suddenly, Burma felt a sickening sensation in her stomach. "I could only find six of my fish," she recalled. "I couldn't believe it. I looked again all over that live well, but that's all I had in it—six. I guess I lost count somewhere along the line and tossed one back in the water when I shouldn't have. I thought I had seven, when I only had six. That meant that I could have kept another one of those bass that I had released.

"I felt pretty stupid—but not nearly as stupid as I felt a little while later."

That's because Burma missed winning some prize money by only one ounce!

"Any one of those bass that I had released would have given me a nice check," she lamented. "You'd think a grown woman would be able to count to seven. Well, I can now. I've never made that mistake again."

Kathy Magers

Truman Reservoir, Missouri, 1984

Kathy Magers tried to use a little brain power to help her in a Bass'n Gal tournament. But for a brief moment her brain short-circuited and left her awash in embarrassment.

"I was fishing a tournament on Truman Reservoir in Missouri," Magers recalled. "It's a manmade reservoir, and that makes a difference whether the water is rising or falling because it will change the places the bass will be."

Magers thought the water was dropping slightly, so when she came back to the marina at the end of the first day, she took a marking pen out and made a mark on the side of the dock. That way she could just check the mark the next morning and immediately know if the water had gone up or down during the night, and by how much.

The next morning Magers was silently congratulating herself on her professionalism as she arrived at the dock and checked the mark. It would reveal vital information that could give her the jump on the other competitors.

To her befuddlement Magers discovered that the water was at the exact same level. She studied the mark again—it was right at the water's edge, where she had put it the day before.

"I was sure the water level was changing and I couldn't understand it," she said. "I looked again. No mistake—the water was even with that mark.

"Then it dawned on me—it was a floating dock!

"Of course, the mark was still at the water level, and it always would be. I felt really klutzy.

"But it could have been worse—at least nobody saw me."

Cliff McKendree
Lake Seminole, Georgia, 1983

When Cliff McKendree tried to catch a newly sharpened fishing lure that he had dropped, he reacted without thinking and got snared in an embarrassing ordeal.

Not to mention a very painful one.

McKendree, a pro bass angler who has won tournaments on several different circuits, was competing in a U.S. Bass Tournament on Lake Seminole. He and fellow pro Bernie Schultz had rented a house trailer to stay in during the event. As most pro anglers do the night before a tournament, the pair were busy going over their tackle—changing lines, checking reel drags, and sharpening hooks. Especially sharpening hooks.

"I was carefully putting the finishing touches on the treble hooks of my favorite crankbait," McKendree recalled. "Those hooks were razor sharp. I was thinking how ready that baby would be for the next day, when suddenly it slipped out of my hand. I didn't want the bait to hit the carpet, because I knew it would really get stuck and be hard to get out."

So, without thinking of the consequences, McKendree made a quick grab for the crankbait. He caught it as it fell—and buried a set of treble hooks in his right wrist.

The pain was so great that McKendree instinctively made a grab at the crankbait with his left hand—and buried the other set of treble hooks in his hand.

"There I was, sitting in pain, handcuffed by that crankbait," McKendree recalled. I couldn't move. . . . I couldn't push my hands together or pull them apart."

Fortunately for McKendree, Schultz was in the room. He managed to free the lure from the hooks, and then very gingerly pulled the hooks out of McKendree's right wrist and left hand. The emergency extraction took about an hour.

"And I swear that whole time I had to listen to Bernie laugh," McKendree said. "He won't let me forget it to this day.

"And almost as bad as the pain was knowing I had spent an hour sharpening those hooks. I still intended to use that bait the next day. So I had to put new hooks on it and sharpen them all over again.

"But this time I was a lot more careful."

Vojai Reed

Broken Bow Lake, Oklahoma, 1984

For lady pro Vojai Reed, it seemed like the perfect tournament. It was on her home lake, her friends and family were watching, and she was one of the favorites to win.

What could possibly go wrong?

Well, for starters, she experienced one of the most shameful starts in a women's tournament.

It happened in 1984 at the Bass'n Gal tournament on Broken Bow Lake, Oklahoma. "I was one of the favorites, since it was a lake I knew so well and I was determined to do my best to live up to that," Reed said. "I wanted to do everything just right."

On the contest's opening morning tournament director Bob Ferris gave the order, "Ladies, start your engines." But Reed's wouldn't start.

"I started to panic," she admitted. "I knew I still had time before they called my flight of boats, so I put the trolling motor over the side and headed for the shore, where my husband, Charlie, and a service crew were standing. I could hear Bob Ferris calling off the contestants' numbers and sending them out, and my heart went right into my throat because I didn't want to miss my start.

"I started to panic even more. As I neared my husband, I just started yelling, 'Get me a service crew!' 'Get me an engine that works!' Everybody along the bank was looking at me, but I didn't care, I was desperate.

"Then someone on the bank—apparently one of the spectators—yelled out, 'Check your kill switch!'

"I died right there. I looked down and there was my kill

switch dangling from my life jacket." Somehow, the kill switch had become disconnected and Reed was so flustered over her apparent engine failure that she failed to notice how simple the problem was. All she had to do was plug in the kill switch.

A kill switch is a device that automatically kills the engine if it is pulled out of a plug on the boat's console. It's common on newer boats today. And in bass tournaments it's mandatory to have the kill switch connected to the life jacket of the boat's driver. That way, if the driver is thrown from the boat, the engine will automatically stop. If the switch is not in its plug, the engine won't start.

"I felt so foolish," Reed recalled. "There was my husband on the bank still waving his arms and frantically yelling for a service crew. There were spectators all over the bank—my hometown fans, many of whom I knew—looking at me standing there with a kill switch in my hand.

"I wish I could have found some way out—some kind of distraction to fool them. But there was no way out. I connected the switch, hit the engine, and roared out of there. I only hoped that I was far enough away from the bank that they couldn't see how red my face was."

Harold Rogers

Lake Lanier, Georgia, 1977

Fishermen have a language all their own. But sometimes when a saltwater angler teams up with a freshwater angler, they speak in different dialects. In other words, what we have here is a failure to communicate.

That's what happened when Harold Rogers went bass fishing with Bud Emery at Lake Lanier in Georgia in 1977. Rogers, of Atlanta, fished mainly in salt water and knew nothing about bass fishing, while Emery was an experienced bass fisherman from Savannah, Georgia.

After motoring out onto the lake Emery gave Rogers a crash course on largemouth-bass fishing and how to use plastic worms to catch them. When he was finished, Emery handed his friend a big bag of plastic worms and said, "Here, you'd better toss out a bunch of worms." Then Emery turned his back and went fishing.

What Emery meant by "tossing out a bunch of worms" was to shake a few plastic worms out of the bag—which had about a hundred in it—and place them nearby in the boat. That way they would be handy whenever the anglers needed another plastic worm.

But Rogers didn't know that. He knew something about chumming, the practice of throwing pieces of cut fish or bait over the side in salt water to attract fish. So Rogers followed Emery's orders to the letter. He "tossed out a bunch of worms" —handfuls of them, in fact—over the side.

All of a sudden Emery noticed plastic worms floating by the bow of the boat and then sinking slowly, one after the other. He looked back to see Rogers launch another handful.

"What are you doing?" Emery shouted.

"I'm tossing out a bunch of plastic worms like you said," replied Rogers.

What Emery said next is unprintable—but, fortunately, the two are still friends.

Jancie Cheek
Lake Eufaula, Alabama, 1981

Top woman angler Jancie Cheek got caught with her pants down.

In 1981 Cheek was fishing the Bass'n Gal Classic at Lake Eufaula, Alabama. Because it was such a prestigious event, tournament officials arranged to have the fishing action filmed for a television show. They gave the film crew carte blanche on where to shoot and told all the competitors to act like professionals. "The officials didn't want us to do something stupid or embarrassing," recalled Cheek.

The chances of that happening seemed remote. After all, the women in the Classic were all professional and knew exactly how to behave and, of course, how to fish.

During the tourney Cheek was running her boat across the lake, intently following her map, when she inadvertently strayed outside the channel. "This lake has a lot of ledges and sandbars on it, and I plowed right up on top of a bar," Cheek recalled. "There I was, high and dry. Fortunately, I thought, there were no camera boats around to film my fiasco.

"So I got out of the boat and pushed it off the bar into deeper water and then got back in. By then my pants were all wet and clammy, so I figured I'd take them off and dry them out." But first she wanted to make doubly sure that she was totally alone. She looked left . . . right . . . backward . . . and forward.

"Since I didn't see anybody around filming, I took off my pants and laid them over a seat to dry," Cheek said. "Then I put on a pair of rain pants. I think they belonged to my husband, because they were big and bulky. I must have looked like some kind of old farm girl standing up there in the boat with those things on."

Cheek went ahead and fished the rest of the day without incident. Not until she returned to the ramp did she learn that she had not been alone.

"What I didn't know was that everything I did had been filmed—by an airplane overhead!" Cheek said. "They filmed me pushing the boat off the bar, changing my pants, draping my pants out to dry, everything.

"Fortunately they never used the footage on TV—but they made sure that I knew they had it. It's pretty unsettling knowing that film is lying around somewhere."

Al McClane and Arnold Gingrich

Upstate New York, 1968

Two legendary New York City fly fishermen cast their own version of dry fly fishing that went from the ridiculous to the sublime.

A. J. "Al" McClane, longtime angling editor of *Field and Stream* magazine, and the late Arnold Gingrich, editor of *Esquire,* were good friends. They were also two of the most famous fishermen from Manhattan, and probably the whole country, in the nineteen sixties.

Gingrich had a small getaway home in upstate New York, about three hours from the city, that featured a trout pond on the property. One January day in 1968 he invited McClane to join him at the cabin for a weekend.

McClane jumped at the chance for a respite from the hectic Big Apple grind. The two left on a cold winter Friday evening and arrived at the cabin a few hours later. The first thing the two old friends did was down a few drinks in front of the fireplace. Then they had a few more drinks.

Of course, they talked about fishing, and it wasn't long before Gingrich invited McClane to go outside and try their luck casting for trout. "Great," said McClane. The two men rigged up their fly rods, bundled up, brought a few more liquid refreshments with them, and trekked down to the pond.

Soon both men were fly-casting out into the dark moonless night. Each man was expertly working his rod back and forth, artistically presenting his fly.

"Isn't this the life?" beamed Gingrich.

McClane nodded in agreement. But something was troubling him. He turned to Gingrich and said, "You know, Arnold, there's something wrong here. It just doesn't feel right." He cast again and then peered intently out at the pond. Suddenly, he thought he had discovered the answer.

"My God, Arnold," said the thunderstruck McClane. "I think the pond's frozen!" Then he looked a little harder. "Damn, I know the pond's iced over. Arnold, we're trying to catch trout from a frozen pond!"

Gingrich looked disdainfully at his old buddy. "Well, of course the pond's frozen," he snapped. "It's winter, you dummy. But it sure beats the hell out of anything we could be doing back in New York."

McClane pondered his friend's words for a moment and replied, "Yes, you're absolutely right." With that said, the pair returned to their number-one passion—fly casting.

BY HOOK
OR
BY CROOK

The Sneakiest
Cases of
Fishing Violations

Mrs. "Fanny Fish"

Gunnison River, Colorado, 1958

In one of the silliest and slimiest cases ever of hiding evidence, a woman poacher stuffed freshly caught fish in her underwear in the hopes of tricking authorities. But they got to the bottom of her chicanery.

The case of Mrs. "Fanny Fish" unfolded in the upper Gunnison River, which was famous for its abundant trout, particularly in June when the mayflies hatched. Fishermen came from all over the country when the hatch was on.

Game wardens flocked there, too, to keep an eye out for violators.

Colorado wildlife officer Clyde Slonaker, using a common and well-known tactic, set up a roadblock on U.S. Highway 50 to spot-check fishermen. He also stationed a warden ahead of the checkpoint to look for drivers who attempted to turn around when they saw the checkpoint warning sign.

One day in 1958, late in the afternoon, the lookout saw a car pull off the road and turn around. The officer quickly raced after the car, stopping it before it could get away. He looked inside and saw a man who still had his fishing boots on, fishing gear in sight, and a wicker creel in the seat between him and his wife. The officer checked the man's license and asked him to pull over at the checkpoint for a more thorough search. Two wardens searched the car and found that the couple had the legal limit of fish. Absolutely nothing seemed to be wrong.

"But the lookout officer came up to me and said he was sure there had to be something fishy going on with this couple because the driver had attempted to escape the checkpoint," Slonaker recalled. "Besides, there seemed to be a lot of fish slime, scales, and river grass on the front seat, as though they had counted fish there. And the officer was positive they hadn't been able to throw any fish out of the car before he stopped them.

"The only other odd thing was that the woman had refused to get out of the front seat. I asked her to please step out so we could get a better look under the seat. Her husband answered that she could not walk. So I asked, 'How does she get in and out, then?' And he said, 'She uses a wheelchair.' That would have seemed reasonable except that the woman's shoes were on the floor of the car and they clearly showed a lot of walking wear. So I tried to trip her up. I asked her if her wheelchair was a right- or left-hand drive. And she looked blank. I told her we really needed her to get out of the car, and if she wouldn't step out willingly, we'd forcibly remove her."

The woman, who was quite hefty, reluctantly stepped out and another officer quickly looked under the front seat—but found nothing. However, Slonaker noticed she was standing awfully rigid—and both the seat and her pants were quite wet. When he asked her to move away from the car, a horrified look came over her face.

"She took one step and a trout slid out from under her pants . . . another step, and another trout slid out," Slonaker recalled. "These trout were still fresh, wet and slick and probably pretty cold. As we walked her back and forth, fourteen more trout, all ten to fourteen inches long, slipped out of her pants. We now had sixteen trout.

"Those last few trout were mighty slow in coming out, so we weren't sure we had got them all or not. In those days there were no female officers, so I asked her to walk some more. Finally, I asked her to lean over and, sure enough, there was a clear imprint of a trout on her rear end. The trout had stuck there when she sat on it.

"I asked her to remove it and she refused. Well, like I say, we didn't have any female officers, so I just charged them with having seventeen trout over the limit. The lady never said a word. She just got back in the car with the trout still stuck to her underwear and stared straight ahead.

"I gave her husband a court summons and when we last saw the pair drive away, she was still sitting on that trout."

Apparently, Mrs. "Fanny Fish" was hoping to put the whole fishy mess behind her.

Mr. "Tough Luck"

Lake Erie, Ohio, 1987

An angler known as Mr. "Tough Luck" discovered that too much good luck can be a bad thing. In fact, it can be downright criminal.

He was fishing with a buddy on Lake Erie off the Toledo shoreline. It was a beautiful, crisp fall afternoon that had lured just about every perch angler in Toledo out onto the lake.

Among the two hundred or so boats on the water was one owned by Ohio wildlife officer Terry Sunderhaus, who was off duty and out of uniform. He was fishing with his father-in-law, Ted Davies, in a little sixteen-foot boat, and both were hoping to catch their share of yellow perch.

They weren't having nearly the good fortune that Tough Luck was enjoying about a half mile away. The lucky stiff was pulling in perch just as fast as he could stick his line in the water. His luck was so good that he had caught nearly double the legal limit of fifty perch. Meanwhile, his friend had pulled in another thirty perch.

"We better give some of them away before we get back," Tough Luck said to his pal. "We don't want to run the risk of the game warden catching us." Gazing at the boats on the lake, he pointed to a small sixteen-footer and said, "How about giving some of our fish to those guys in that boat over there?"

And that's when his luck turned bad—because, of the hundreds of boats on the lake, he had picked out the only one with an off-duty wildlife officer aboard!

Tough Luck ran his boat over to Sunderhaus and told him, "I have way over the limit. Can you take some off my hands? That damn game warden always sits by the boat ramp and I don't want to take any chances."

"Sure," said Sunderhaus, stunned by the incredible odds of having an offender choose his boat. The angler handed Sunderhaus thirty yellow perch.

Tough Luck then accepted Sunderhaus's offer of having a beer with him on the lake. The officer was friendly only because he needed time to note the boat registration so he could bust the angler later for taking more than the limit.

After sharing a brew with Sunderhaus, Tough Luck headed for shore, congratulating himself on his good luck at catching so many perch. He had no problem with the game warden at the ramp and went home a happy fisherman.

But Tough Luck wasn't so happy the next day when Sunderhaus showed up at his door—in uniform. "Remember me?" Sunderhaus asked him.

"Oh, no," moaned the flabbergasted angler. "You mean to tell me that of all those boats, I picked you? What rotten luck!" Tough Luck, who was fined a hundred dollars plus court costs, didn't fight the charge because, he told Sunderhaus, "I was wrong and I got caught. Besides, anyone with my kind of luck deserves to get punished."

Flat Brook Valley Club

Big Flat Brook, New Jersey, 1911

An exclusive trout club for the rich shamelessly tried to hoard all the fish for its own enjoyment. But the club netted nothing but trouble from local anglers.

In 1911 the Flat Brook Valley Club bought twelve miles of a northwest New Jersey trout stream called Big Flat Brook. The acquisition angered the local fishermen, who had been catching trout in Flat Brook for years to feed their families. Even more infuriating, the club—made up entirely of people from outside the area—fenced off the stream. The club then posted NO TRESPASSING signs to keep the locals from poaching trout.

The battle lines were drawn. And it was Wilbur Hamler's job to defend the club's waters from the army of angry anglers. As the club caretaker, Hamler took his duties very seriously. He allowed no one but members and guests to fish the club waters, which included a pond stocked with giant trout. While Hamler was on the job, poaching was almost impossible.

After a couple of years Hamler noticed that the cold war between the club and the community appeared to have thawed. He even took up an invitation to join a weekly poker game that some of the local good old boys had started. Hamler happily played cards with them for several years.

But one day it dawned on him that at every game, there was always at least one cardplayer missing. His suspicions aroused, Hamler launched an investigation and discovered that his "friends" had arranged the poker games for one purpose only. They had Hamler completely occupied at the card table to guarantee one of their buddies an evening of unmolested poaching at Big Flat Brook.

Needless to say, Hamler quit the poker game.

But the locals weren't the only ones who poached. The club members themselves were greedily stealing trout from the public sections of the stream. The club had erected a dam at its southern boundary to insure that the big trout it stocked wouldn't escape into public waters. But several members were seen standing on the dam catching the little trout below the dam in public waters and then releasing them in club waters on the other side.

The game warden quickly put a stop to that. But that wasn't good enough for the locals. Such an affront couldn't go unpunished. And it didn't. One night someone sneaked in and dynamited the dam!

That was the beginning of the end for the club. It gradually declined in membership and eventually was bought by the state. Today, the fishing's not as good—but it's all in public water.

Ski Bum

Eagle River, Colorado, 1984

A ski bum discovered that skiing and fishing don't mix—especially out of season.

One spring day in 1984 near Vail, Colorado, wildlife officer Bill Andree was walking along the Eagle River looking for fishing violations. Suddenly, he stopped in his tracks when he noticed in the distance what looked like a skier waving something on the river.

"I watched this guy through binoculars," Andree said. "He was waving what looked like a ski pole, back and forth, back and forth. I couldn't figure it out. I thought maybe he was signaling to somebody. The last thing I thought he was doing was fishing."

But when Andree went down to the banks of the river and approached the man, he could see the man had a fly reel taped onto a ski pole.

It was a ski bum fly-fishing . . . with a ski pole!

"He had a dry fly on the end of the line and was whipping it back and forth as best he could," Andree recalled. "He even had a fishing vest on.

"I asked him what in the world he was doing fly-fishing with a ski pole, and he explained that he was a ski bum who had come to Vail for the skiing. But the skiing wasn't the best because of the melting snow. He had cabin fever and wanted to get away from the slopes. He liked to fish but didn't have a fishing rod with him, so he improvised."

"Unfortunately for him, he hadn't improvised a fishing license, so it cost him fifty dollars. And the worst thing was that he hadn't caught any fish with his ski pole either."

Fish Pirates
Lake Rodríguez, Mexico, 1985

In one of the most bizarre raids in the annals of fishing, three pirates swam out to the canoe of bass angler Bernie Kuhel and robbed him not of jewels or money . . . but of his bass!

The San Diego angler was fishing from a canoe in Lake Rodríguez near Tijuana, Mexico, in 1985 when his scary encounter took place. Brazen bandits were hardly on Kuhel's mind as he enjoyed the peaceful pursuit of bass.

"I was fishing in a cove and within an hour I'd caught four nice two- to three-pound bass on plastic worms," he recalled. "All of a sudden three guys were hanging on the side of my canoe! They'd swum out from the shore and were looking at me eyeball to eyeball. I couldn't believe it.

"They didn't speak any English, just Spanish, which I didn't understand, but they made it clear that they wanted my fish. With them hanging on the side of my canoe and it starting to tip, I didn't have much in the way of options. I gave them the fish."

Unlike the pirates of old the fish filchers didn't swim away with cutlasses in their teeth. They had their chompers firmly clamped on the fish instead. "That was the most unbelievable part," said Kuhel. "The fish were alive and squirming, and these guys bit down on the bass so they could have their hands free for swimming.

"They swam back to shore. The last I saw of them, they had a fire going and were starting to cook fish tacos.

"The whole thing was really bizarre. I'd been fishing Lake Rodríguez regularly for a couple of years and never had anything like that happen before."

The bass-booty buccaneers were believed to be local rowdies who were either too lazy to fish for themselves or else didn't have any fishing equipment—a nasty band of Captain Hooklesses.

Despite his frightening experience Kuhel vowed to go fishing again on Lake Rodríguez. But just in case he ran into those same pirates again, he enrolled in a Spanish class so he could give them a piece of his mind in their native tongue.

Tony Faulk

Lake Tyler, Texas, 1988

Tony Faulk landed the biggest catfish ever caught in the state of Texas, a 122-pound behemoth with a mouth one and a half feet wide. But don't look for Faulk's name in the record books—check court records instead.

That's because the angler was arrested and fined for catching the monster illegally.

And Faulk puts all the blame on the "bigmouth." Not the fish but Faulk himself. He bragged a little too much to his buddies about just how he had caught the big cat.

Faulk spotted the incredibly huge flathead catfish, which was an estimated seventy years old, beneath a dock on Lake Tyler, Texas, about eight P.M. one evening in 1988.

Instead of using a hook and line, Faulk just couldn't resist using his hands to try wrestling the slow-moving catfish. Taking catfish by hand—a technique called "grappling"—was against the law in that state.

Faulk sneaked up behind the fish and grabbed it by the gills, then threw a rope around its fat body. He tugged Old Bigmouth onto the bank, tussled with it until he finally got it into the trunk of his car, and sped into town. There, he gave all his pals a minute-by-minute account of the wrestling match and then showed them his amazing catch—which weighed eight pounds more than the Texas record of 114 pounds.

It wasn't long before game warden Jerry Chilton got wind of the angler's offense. Chilton arrested Faulk just as he was about to fillet Old Bigmouth.

"It turned into a catastrophe," lamented Faulk.

His big mouth had cost him a prize fish, a $125 fine—and a spot in the state record books.

Said Judge Bill Beaird, who heard the case: "If he'd kept his mouth shut, he probably wouldn't have been caught."

Disquieting Disqualifications

Unfortunately, tournaments are occasionally plagued with cheaters who will resort to desperate and shameful measures. For example:

● Brothers John and Archie Wade were disqualified from first and second place in a big bass tournament on Lake Wright Patman in Texas in 1983.

Officials became suspicious because the "winning" twelve-pound-plus bass was two pounds bigger than anything ever caught in the lake before. And the second-place bass was close to the previous record as well. Besides that, both fish were brought to the weigh-in dead, already rotting and stinking. When the two brothers flunked lie-detector tests, they were DQ'ed.

● Garry Wayne Parkerson, a paroled marijuana farmer, collected a $105,000 prize for his big bass in a Texas tournament in 1983. But police in his home area of Webster Parish, Louisiana, were suspicious of his good fortune. "We knew he didn't even fish," explained Det. O. H. Hayes.

When they raided his home some weeks later on another criminal matter, police found fourteen huge bass swimming around in a small artificial pond in his backyard. Parkerson said he kept the eight-pound-sized bass "for food." But he eventually pleaded guilty in federal court to intent to defraud as part of a ring that brought Florida bass to Texas tournaments.

● In Pembroke, Massachusetts, in 1985, brothers Richard and David Bernier of Middleboro, Massachusetts, were disqualified from a bass tournament after five live bass were found in their live well—before the tournament even started!

● In Port Angeles, Washington, William and Joan Parks tried to claim first and second prize in the 1981 Port Angeles Salmon Derby—with fish that had previously been frozen.

Their thawing of the fish was so inept that tournament organizers didn't even have to resort to lie detectors or sophisticated scientific instruments to detect the fraud—local fishermen just hooted at their forty-three- and thirty-six-pound salmon when they saw them. The couple were arrested immediately.

Later, in court, the third-place finisher confessed that his fish, too, had been frozen and given to him by the Parkses.

• In a Freeport, Texas, saltwater tournament, an angler and his girlfriend cheated twice in three days.

Their first attempt to nail a prize was with a four-pound flounder—but it was disqualified after tests indicated it had been frozen. That didn't stop the pair. They then produced a red drum that weighed eight pounds and was a potential first-place fish . . . until lead sinkers were found in its stomach.

Officials were so disgusted with the couple's chicanery that they put up a special category on the leader board of the three-day tournament headed "cheaters."

• At the Havana Marlin Tournament in Cuba in 1940, competitors were suspicious of the back-to-back tourney wins of a wealthy angler. So they hired a spy who tailed the fisherman.

The spy followed the suspect's boat as it drifted away from the tournament fleet and put into port at Cojimar, a small commercial fishing village near Havana. The angler then bought a marlin from one of the commercial boats. He did the same thing the following day.

But when he came out of the harbor's narrow entrance, he was stunned to find his devious shame exposed. The entire fleet was lined up on both sides of the channel. As the cheater ran the gauntlet, the boats all blared their horns and the competitors booed in derision.

Ole Paulson

Nestoria Township, Michigan, 1937

Justice in Michigan's Upper Peninsula a half century ago
was as wild as a whitewater river. An outsider never knew
what to expect. But a local poacher knew swimmingly well
how to beat the system.

To District Attorney John Voelker it looked like an open-
and-shut case. Ole Paulson of Nestoria Township was charged
with catching forty-seven brook trout out of season with a net.
He pleaded not guilty and the case was set for trial before a
justice of the peace who just happened to have the same name
and live in the same township as the defendant.

It wasn't all that unusual for people here to have the same
name, because the area was inhabited mostly by Swedish im-
migrants, many of whom were related to each other.

Voelker decided to try the case rather than send an assis-
tant, because he was dying to find out precisely where a man
could ever *find* forty-seven brook trout in one place, regardless
of how he took them. Voelker, an avid fisherman, recounted
the trial in his book *Trout Madness,* which he wrote under
the pen name of Robert Traver.

The courtroom was a high-ceilinged, plaster-falling cham-
ber from which the Honorable Ole Paulson sold insurance,
game and fish licenses, live bait, and sundry bottled goods.

The courtroom was crowded. Every adult male in the community had forsaken the village tavern for a few hours and
moved across the street for the trial.

Voelker met with the prosecution's star witness, an eager
young conservation officer named Clark, who had arrested the
defendant. The officer told the D.A. that the list of the six jurors had been prepared by Deputy Sheriff Paulson. "It has not
escaped my notice that I seem to be getting fairly well hemmed
in by Paulsons," Voelker told Clark.

His Honor then banged the desk with a gavel made from a
hammer wrapped in an old sock. "Yentleman of da yury," Justice Paulson said, "you vill now go sit over dare." Six local
jurors scrambled for their seats. Next, Paulson jammed a fresh
wad of tobacco in his cheeks and began spitting a stream into

a brass cuspidor. Finally, he ordered Voelker to call his first witness.

Conservation Officer Clark testified that he had seen the defendant, Ole Paulson, lifting a net from Nestoria Creek. The officer said he'd confiscated forty-seven brook trout, which were now being kept in a freezer in the tavern across the street from the courtroom. After a brief recess, the net and the fish were retrieved from the tavern and introduced as evidence.

Then it was the defendant's turn. Ole Paulson testified that he had been merely patrolling the creek looking for beaver signs for the next trapping season when he came across the illegal net. He claimed the net wasn't his, nor had he set it. Paulson stated that he was just lifting the net to free the unfortunate trout and destroy the net when the conservation officer arrived and arrested him. "Dat's all dere vas to it!" Paulson declared.

Voelker pointed out the absurdity of the defendant's story. Why would Paulson be prowling a trout stream in mid-September looking for beaver signs for a trapping season that didn't open until the following March? For his closing argument Voelker reminded the jury that a poacher was no different from a thief stealing the people's tax money; that fish and game belonged to *all* the people.

Paulson's closing statement was brief. Pointing scornfully at the fish net, he said, "Yentleman of da yury. Who da heck's ever seen a good Svede using vun of dem gol-dang homemade Finlander nets? I tank you!"

The jury deliberated for as long as it felt necessary—about two minutes. Then the foreman announced: "Ve find da defendant not guilty!"

The crowd cheered and hustled off to the tavern across the street to celebrate Ole Paulson's acquittal. Only then did Voelker glance at the six-man jury list: Ragnar Paulson, Swan Paulson, Luther Paulson, Eskil Paulson, Incher Paulson, and Magnus Carl Magnuson.

Voelker turned to Deputy Sheriff Paulson and asked, "How did Magnuson ever get on this jury list?"

Paulson shrugged. "Ve yust simply ran out of Paulsons. Anyvay, Magnuson is my son's brudder-in-law. My son is da defendant, you know."

Voelker shook his head in resignation and walked over to the tavern. He banged his fist on the bar and shouted in a mock Swedish accent, "Giff all da Paulsons in da place vatever dey vant!"

Caught Unaware

An illegal angler caught the worst thing imaginable—he hooked the local game warden.

Colorado wildlife officer Rick Spowart was out of uniform and kayaking down the Blue River in a section for flies and artificial lures only. As he glided around a sharp bend in the river, the bow of his kayak got hooked on the line of a fisherman who was on the bank. Dangling off the hook was a big night-crawler.

"The man was quite belligerent and very annoyed that I had interfered with his fishing," Spowart recalled. "As I paddled in, I noticed he was standing right next to a sign which proclaimed that this was a flies-and-lures-only section of the river.

"I identified myself and immediately charged him with fishing illegally, which was a sixty-eight-dollar fine. There wasn't much he could say. He had hooked my kayak with a night crawler. And he couldn't very well say he couldn't read the sign next to him—because he was a school teacher."

Chris McCants

Walt Disney World, Florida, 1990

Fifteen-year-old Chris McCants was a Mickey Mouse fisherman until he got caught for some Goofy angling at Walt Disney World.

In 1990 the West Palm Beach, Florida, teenager was staying with his parents at the Buena Vista Palace Hotel overlooking Buena Vista Lagoon in the Walt Disney World Shopping Village. Chris, who loved to fish and had brought along his fishing gear, noticed that the lake was full of bass, bluegill, and gar. So he went down to the bank and began fishing until a hotel official informed him that he couldn't fish there.

Not wanting to break any rules, Chris took his rod and reel and went back to his hotel room. Then it dawned on him that although the hotel official told him he couldn't fish from the bank, nothing was said about not fishing from the balcony outside his tenth-floor hotel room.

So Chris went out onto the balcony and dropped his line down. Within ten minutes he'd hooked a bluegill, and reeled it up to the tenth floor. Then he caught two more bluegill. He released all three by dropping them from the balcony back into the lake. Chris also hooked a large bass, which shook loose somewhere around the fourth floor and plopped back into the water.

While his family was admiring his fishing prowess from the balcony, there was a knock on the door. A hotel security man politely informed them that he was investigating some strange reports. Patrons from the ground-floor restaurant claimed that while looking outside the restaurant they spotted fish seemingly going up and then going down past the window.

The security officer hadn't wanted to believe the diners at first. But then he noticed the fishing line dangling from the balcony and followed it to Chris's room. The teen angler readily admitted that he had been fishing from the tenth floor. When told that fishing was a no-no, Chris put away his rod and reel and ended his high angling adventure.

Beer Bottle Arm
Florida Keys, 1968

A lamebrained angler who threw a beer bottle at a passing boater quickly found himself on the wrong end of a fishing pole.

In 1968 Jim Strader, who today owns Strader Lures, was working as a guide in the Florida Keys, a chain of islands connected by bridges. Most of the bridges span water where there are plenty of fish and definite channels for boaters to use. Most fishermen are knowledgeable enough not to fish from any bridge above the middle of a channel.

Most, but not all.

One day Strader was motoring back from the ocean along the channel under a U.S. Highway 1 bridge. He had just cleared the bridge when . . . BAM! . . . a beer bottle smashed down on the deck of his boat. Glass flew everywhere, but fortunately, Strader was not hurt. Once the shock of the unpleasant surprise wore off, Strader's anger began to build.

He wanted to find the jerk who had thrown the bottle. So Strader turned his boat around and scanned the top of the bridge. Then he spotted the culprit—a heavyset sunburned cretin who was yelling and making obscene gestures at him for lousing up his fishing. Never mind that the lunkhead shouldn't have been fishing above the channel.

By now the fuming-mad Strader was heading back toward the bridge. He didn't know what he was going to do, but he knew he was going to get even. Although Strader was a husky man—well over two hundred pounds—he didn't want to get into a fight. No, he wanted a revenge that would teach Beer Bottle Arm a lesson he'd never forget.

As the boat neared the bridge, Strader sized up the scene. Beer Bottle Arm was decked out in a gigantic shark-fishing outfit. He was wearing a shoulder harness like a vest with a huge rod and reel attached to it with clips. Strader knew there was no fast, easy way for Beer Bottle Arm to get out of this setup. Then he noticed that the fathead's fishing line—a heavy fifty-pound test—was dangling in the water.

Suddenly, Strader had a brainstorm. A smile crept across

76

his lips and he felt a tingle of anticipation—the kind he got whenever he set the hook on a tarpon.

Ignoring Beer Bottle Arm's ranting and raving from above, Strader guided his boat up to the fishing line. Without saying a word Strader grabbed the line and wrapped it a half-dozen times around a cleat on his boat. Then he whipped the boat around, gunned it—and zoomed off.

He looked back when he was about a hundred yards away. On the bridge Beer Bottle Arm was fighting mightily to keep from being yanked off the bridge. With his rod bent over, the line was flying off his reel, and since he was still attached to his rod, he was helpless to do anything but hang on for dear life—and bellow curses.

Strader never looked back again. When he arrived at his home marina, he found plenty of line trailing off his cleat. It had either snapped or been cut by Beer Bottle Arm.

Somewhere, hoped Strader, there's a wiser fisherman who will think twice before throwing a beer bottle at a boater.

Kermit Haugen

Yellowstone National Park, 1984

It started out as a simple illegal fishing incident. But before it was over, it involved nationwide headlines, an appearance on *Donahue,* a multimillion-dollar lawsuit, and a court case that stretched out for almost two years.

In 1984 Marc Glines, a Yellowstone National Park ranger, was on routine patrol when he spotted Kermit Haugen fishing on the Firehole River with a spinning rod. That particular river was for fly fishing only. As Glines approached the angler, he noticed a foam container of worms at Haugen's feet. It was illegal to use live bait, including worms, anywhere in Yellowstone.

"I asked him if he was having any luck and he said no, but he'd had a few nibbles," Glines recalled. "He then reeled in his line and his hook had a night crawler on it. I told him I was a park ranger and asked to see his fishing permit. He said he didn't need one."

When Glines told him the stream was fly fishing only, that everyone needed a special park permit to fish, and that live bait was illegal in Yellowstone, Haugen said he was unaware of all that.

"To get where he was, he had to have passed at least fifteen signs stating the rules and that the Firehole was fly fishing only," Glines recalled. "I wasn't impressed with his answer."

Usually in such cases the ranger will inform the violator of the rules, order him to stop fishing, and ask to see some form of identification. Glines asked Haugen for his driver's license.

"He said he didn't have one because he didn't need one," recalled the ranger. "When I asked him how he got to the river, he said he drove and pointed to a truck. That's when I first knew this was going to be a long day. I just didn't know how long."

Glines asked Haugen several times for his date of birth and some kind of ID. Each time Haugen refused to answer, stating it violated his constitutional rights.

The ranger then walked over to Haugen's truck to get the license-plate number. But there was no license plate. When Glines asked him why, Haugen said he didn't need one. What he did have on his truck was a plate that read, IN GOD I TRUST. Next, Glines asked him for his truck registration and Haugen said he hadn't registered it—because he didn't need one.

"Mr. Haugen was a member of a fringe group that had a very rigid view of the Constitution," said Glines. "He made it clear that he did not believe in the government's right to license a citizen's activities.

"I cited him anyway—for fishing with worms in a fly-fishing-only area and for failure to register his vehicle. I could have taken him to jail, but I gave him a break and told him to appear in court the next day."

In court Haugen refused to plead guilty or not guilty, so the magistrate entered a not-guilty plea and set up a jury trial for him in district court. Haugen then told the magistrate that he did not believe in the bar association and he would represent himself.

Although Haugen could have entered a guilty plea and paid a hundred-dollar fine, he chose to fight in court. He was found guilty and the judge sentenced him to sixty days in jail and fined him one thousand dollars plus court costs.

Haugen then began flooding the courts with appeals and other forms of legal briefs. He also sued Glines and the court officials for seventeen million dollars because he claimed his rights had been violated.

"He bombarded us with reams of questions and forms," said Glines. "Every day packets of mail would come in with queries like 'Admit, yes or no—there are no fish in that section of the Firehole River.' "

In all Haugen filed forty separate motions before his case finally ended—with Haugen serving the time and paying the fine.

But the saga wasn't over. Newspapers across the country ran stories about the man "guilty of fishing with a worm." But few papers bothered to delve into the background of Haugen's bizarre behavior and he became something of a celebrity. He appeared on *Donahue,* where he blasted the federal government for its unjust ways.

As for Haugen's seventeen-million-dollar suit, it was thrown out of court like an undersized fish.

Toledo City Water Company Poachers

Toledo, Ohio, 1984

Fish aren't the only ones who should keep their mouths shut if they don't want to get caught—poachers should too.

One fish thief bragged about his crime and witlessly helped authorities net a band of poachers whose illegal operation scandalized the city of Toledo, Ohio.

In 1984 Ohio wildlife officer Terry Sunderhaus went undercover after learning of the poaching ring. Sitting in a bar posing as an installer of automatic chicken feeders, Sunderhaus was lamenting what lousy luck he was having fishing. "I promised my wife I'd bring home some walleye and I didn't catch a thing," he moaned to the patrons.

A stranger on the next stool spoke up. "Too bad about your luck," he said. "You ought to fish with me. I load up on walleyes and perch all the time—and I don't even use a hook."

"No hook?" asked Sunderhaus, who was immediately interested, since almost all of the ways to catch those kinds of fish without a hook are illegal. "How do you do that?"

The bar patron explained in glorious detail. He worked for the City of Toledo Water Company and was part of a sophisticated fish-poaching ring that did its dirty work by the utility's water intake plant off of Lake Erie. Enormous quantities of walleye, perch, and other fish would swim into the intake canal and wind up dead ended at the plant—where the ring had conveniently rigged up a giant metal basket. When the basket was full of fish, an electric hoist would lift it and spill the fish out onto the ground. Then the fish would be cleaned using electric scalers on a large fish-cleaning table set up at the plant. Two electric smokers were on hand for smoking fish as well. Besides the basket, the men used long poles tipped with hooks to snag fish.

"How could such a big operation go on at a public utility without the bosses knowing about it?" Sunderhaus asked innocently.

"It doesn't," replied the poacher. "They know about it. Some are even in on it."

It took a few weeks for Sunderhaus to gain the man's trust. Eventually, the poacher agreed to show Sunderhaus and another undercover wildlife officer the entire setup. At the plant the man lowered the wire basket. When it was full of fish, he raised it and gave the two wildlife officers a few dozen walleye.

A short time later a massive raid was staged on the plant and the wire basket, the smokers, the scalers, the poles, weight scales, and other paraphernalia were seized. Before the investigation was over, more than twenty city employees were arrested and convicted, including a commissioner of the Toledo water utility. Some of the poachers were caught with as much as seventy pounds of walleye fillets in their freezers. Other workers in on the scheme confessed they had delivered fillets to officials around the city. It was one of the most celebrated cases in Ohio wildlife-enforcement history.

So what happened to the stranger in the bar?

"He was caught and convicted," Sunderhaus said. "But he didn't know that he was the cause of the raid. He never realized that the two guys he blabbed to in a bar, and later took on a guided tour of the poaching operation, were wildlife officers."

Sunderhaus never saw the poacher again, and his role in the whole investigation was kept undercover. Until now.

Jimmy Childress

Wild Horse Creek, Oklahoma, 1948

It was Oklahoma's most shocking fishing trip . . . full of mystery, intrigue, crime—and naked bodies.

Fourteen-year-old Jimmy Childress showed up at the doorstep of his cousin, Billy Childress, one evening lugging a large black box and invited him to "go down to Wild Horse Creek and catch us some fish." Billy eagerly accepted. As they walked toward the creek, Billy asked what was in the box.

Jimmy cast him a mysterious glance and launched into a tirade against "noodlers"—people who caught huge catfish by wading in streams, locating the fish with their bare feet, and then grabbing the fish with their hands and wrestling them to the bank. "It's getting so you can't catch any big fish," complained Jimmy. "They've all been noodled out."

Then he patted the black box. "But I got me something here that's gonna turn things around. And I won't even have to wet my feet."

Nearing the creek, they pushed through some brush to a particularly inviting spot where the creek curved around a bend. As Jimmy started to open his mysterious black box, the two boys heard a slight commotion from just beyond the bend. They paused and listened for a second, then decided it must have been a raccoon. Jimmy opened the box.

"Why, that ain't nothing but a telephone," Billy said scornfully.

"Just you wait," replied Jimmy. He handed Billy two wires and said, "Hold 'em." Then he cranked the old telephone like mad. Billy dropped the wires and let out a screech. A triumphant Jimmy explained that the crank telephone generated an electric current. The same current that gave a charge to Billy could be used to knock out every fish in the fishing hole. The telephone method was just as illegal as noodling was, said Jimmy.

After feeding the two wires into the creek, he told Billy, "Crank like hell. Then get ready to grab more fish than you've ever seen in your life."

Sure enough, fish began popping up all over the fishing

hole. But something unexpected happened as well. The boys heard hollering from around the corner . . . excited yelps at first . . . and then angry shouts, mixed with a lot of splashes.

The boys looked at each other but didn't say anything. They just ducked inside some thick brambles, dragging the box in with them. Then they peeked around the bend.

They saw three very angry—and very naked—men storming along the creek bank with clothes in their hands and fire in their eyes. The men were "noodlers" who had been wading in the creek for catfish when they got the "shock" of their lives!

Vermont Legislature

1933–Present

Fishing is a peaceful sport, right? Not in one shame-ridden section of Vermont—where the state legislature allows poor fish to get blown out of the water with monster handguns, high-powered rifles, and even shotguns.

The so-called fishermen literally have a blast, the fish don't have a chance . . . and the most disgusting thing about it is that it's all legal.

Fish *hunting* season arrives each spring in Vermont. From March twenty-fifth to May twenty-fifth the shore of Lake Champlain looks like the set of a Rambo movie as trigger-happy Vermonters—armed to the teeth—descend on the lake in droves. They climb up into trees along the shore, watch for telltale ripples on the lake's steely gray surface, and then . . . BLAM! . . . BLAM! . . . BLAM!

It's like shooting fish in a barrel.

Often entire volleys of gunfire sound around the lake. Now and then a fish rolls belly up to the surface. The ideal shot, say the fish hunters, is one that slams into the water just below a fish and stuns it. That way the bullets won't make mincemeat of the fish and it can be eaten.

But even then the fish seldom get to the dinner table. Hunters can legally shoot only "trash fish" like chain pickerel, carp, gar, bowfin, shad, suckers, and bullheads—most of which taste horrible.

But the hunters don't care. It's the thrill of the kill that's important, they say. They also don't care that sport fish such as yellow perch and walleyes often get caught in the concussions and are killed too. Tough luck, they say.

And so what if the bullets kick up silt that destroys eggs laid by spawning fish? So what if this means the supply of young fish gets depleted? Hey, you can't have everything!

There are hazards for humans too. Hunters occasionally fall out of trees. Bullets have ricocheted off the lake's surface and shattered windows in lakeside homes.

But, amazingly, so far nobody has been seriously injured. So each spring members of the bullet brigade return—just as they've been doing since 1933, when the state legislature made fish hunting legal on Lake Champlain.

Furious antihunting forces managed to get the law revoked in 1969. But there's a saying in the Green Mountain State that goes: "If you want a Vermonter to do something, just tell him he can't." So only a year after the law was revoked, it returned to the books with a bang—and the new law allows hunters to shoot even more species of fish!

"This isn't just fun," avid fish shooter James Bernardin told the press. "This is ritual."

No, James, this is sick.

A
BOATLOAD
OF
TROUBLE

The Most
Ridiculous
Boating Mishaps

Gary Klein

Kissimmee Chain of Lakes, Florida, 1982

Many bass fishermen fish "hay fields," dense patches of aquatic vegetation. But only 1989 B.A.S.S. Angler of the Year Gary Klein fished in a cow pasture.

In 1982 Klein was getting psyched up for a big bass tournament on the Kissimmee Chain of Lakes in Florida. A few days before the tourney he was in Maine, giving a seminar on bass fishing. During a break in the seminar an elderly man who used to live on the Kissimmee Chain offered to give Klein some tips about the area.

"I've never been one to rely on fishing information from people who live on the waters where I fish tournaments," said Klein. "But this one time I couldn't pass it up. The man told me about an old, overgrown, unused canal off one of the smaller lakes. He said he didn't think any of the other competitors would know about it, let alone be able to find it. It sounded like a gold mine to me, so I asked him how to go about finding it."

The elderly angler gave Klein a very precise set of landmarks. He even drew a detailed map showing where Klein should line up his boat by aiming at a certain row of cypress trees, take a bearing, and run right into the canal.

"But he warned me that there was one problem," said Klein. "The water leading to the canal was very, very shallow. The only way to get my boat into the canal was to put it on a high-speed plane and run hard. Once I got across the shallow section, I would enter the old canal where the water level was about ten feet deeper."

The following week Klein arrived in central Florida for the first day of practice for the tournament. He couldn't wait to find this secret fishing hole. Carefully studying the old man's hand-drawn map, Klein eased away from the other competitors and headed his boat toward the forgotten canal.

"The old man told me that I really wouldn't know I was in the canal until I actually got there," recalled Klein. "But I was confident that if I lined up on his landmarks and ran hard, I couldn't miss it.

"Well, I went to the right lake and, sure enough, there was the row of cypress trees just as he had drawn on the map. I lined up on the landmark and let her fly. I ran right through a shallow lily-pad section. Then I ran right through a big patch of tall reeds. Still flying at full speed, I came through the reeds, expecting to break out into the mystery canal. Instead, I wound up in a cow pasture!"

Klein's boat had zoomed out of the lake and slid to a jarring stop smack dab in the middle of a bunch of startled Holsteins. Klein, not knowing whether to laugh or cry, was thankful about one thing. At least no one was around to witness this mortifying moment. "It took me three hours of backbreaking work before I could wrestle the boat back into the lake," he said sheepishly. "I didn't look any further for that canal."

Fat Eagle

Wheeler Dam, Tennessee River, Alabama, 1957

Never let a 350-pound Indian named Fat Eagle pull the anchor—that's what Archie Phillips learned the hard way one day on the Tennessee River.

Archie loved to fish for bass and catfish in the wild tailrace waters below the giant Wheeler Dam on the Tennessee River. Back in the nineteen fifties, he used to rent a wooden boat, put his old 3.5-horsepower Wizard outboard motor on it, chug up to the turbulent waters, and anchor.

One day Archie, his son, Archie Junior, and a buddy from work, Fat Eagle, went fishing below the giant dam. They dropped a multipronged anchor onto the rocks in the tailrace. They wanted to make sure the anchor had a good firm hold against the strong current generated by the dam's turbines.

After they fished the first spot, they decided to move the boat a little farther down the river. When it came time to raise the anchor, young Archie—a seventeen-year-old high-school football player who was proud of his muscle power—grabbed the anchor rope and began to heave. But nothing happened. He tried again but couldn't budge the anchor from the bottom of the tailrace.

Fat Eagle also fancied himself as something of a strongman, and he always felt there wasn't anything he couldn't do. After watching the boy's struggles Fat Eagle growled, "Get out of the way, boy, I'll pull that anchor off the bottom."

So Fat Eagle stood at the bow and heaved . . . and heaved . . . and heaved . . . and still the anchor wouldn't give. But he wasn't about to admit defeat.

In those days the old rental boats had square fronts to them. So Fat Eagle sat down in the bow, braced his legs against the square front, and tugged on that anchor with all his might.

And still it stood fast.

But Fat Eagle wasn't done—not yet. He had a plan. He turned to Archie and said, "Archie, trust me. I'm going to pull this anchor off the bottom. Go ahead and crank up the motor and when I tell you to 'hit it,' throw it into gear and pop it wide open. That'll do it."

That was the plan.

Fat Eagle got back on the deck, braced his legs against the square front of the boat, and got ready to yank at the anchor rope. Archie started the engine and waited for the command.

"Hit it!" yelled Fat Eagle.

So Archie threw the engine into gear and opened it wide. Fat Eagle pushed his legs against the bow and reared his 350 pounds back on the anchor rope—and kicked the whole front of the boat off!

It sank like a stone.

Archie made it to shore about a quarter mile down the river. Fat Eagle managed to struggle to land a half mile downstream. But Archie Junior didn't reach shore until he was swept nearly two miles away from the sinking.

They lost all their rods, reels, and tackle—but they were thankful they still had their lives. And their sense of humor. And their love of fishing.

Archie Phillips continued to fish the tailrace below Wheeler Dam. But, he added, "I never let Fat Eagle pull the anchor again."

John Hale

A Florida Lake, 1971

No matter how many times you trailer a boat, and no matter how good you think you are at it, there comes that time when you forget one little thing. And that's what happened to John Hale.

Hale, now a pro fisherman and fishing-lure manufacturer, was stationed at Fort Rucker, Alabama, in 1971, having just returned from Vietnam. He had a long weekend off, so he decided to join some friends who were camping at a small Florida lake.

Towing his fifteen-foot bass boat with its sixty-horse engine, Hale arrived in the dead of night, three A.M., and decided to launch the boat immediately so he'd be ready to fish at dawn.

But this was a real backwoods ramp—no lights at all. Hale positioned the boat at the top of the ramp, got out, and checked everything thoroughly. Or so he thought. Yes, the straps were taken off the boat. Yes, the transom plug was put in (he was too experienced to forget something as elementary as the plug). Yes, everything was ready to go.

Watching out his rearview mirror and using his backup lights for illumination, Hale backed the boat down and waited for it to float off the trailer. But it didn't move. So he backed it down some more. Still the boat didn't float off. So he backed down just a little bit more.

Clunk.

"I heard this big thud and felt a knock in the rear," he recalled. "But the boat still hadn't come off the trailer. I couldn't understand what had happened. So I looked out the side window and discovered the water level was up to the floor of my car.

"Now I knew what happened. I had forgotten to unhook the boat from the trailer! So no matter how much I backed down, the boat floated all right, but not off the trailer. And I had finally backed right off the ramp.

"I was really stuck. I couldn't go forward because I

couldn't get the trailer over the lip of the ramp. And if I went back any farther, I'd sink the car."

Water kept seeping through the doors. By the time he got out, there were six inches of water in the car. Mortified beyond belief, Hale had to swallow his pride, run to the campground, wake one of his friends, and explain what had happened. His buddy used a three-quarter-ton truck to tow the boat and the slightly submerged car out of the water.

Hale not only had to contend with the water damage to his car, but he also had to face what every angler flirts with when he goes fishing—ridicule. A fisherman's friends live for moments like this, and Hale's were no different.

"To this day," said Hale, "my friends never let me forget about the time I trailered my boat—and launched my car."

Fidel Castro
Lake Redonda, Cuba, 1978

Cuban dictator Fidel Castro invited a group of American outdoor writers to his country for a fishing outing in hopes of improving relations between the two countries.

But Castro's plans backfired . . . because that's what his outboard motors did. Time and time again. In fact, they were so terrible, so unreliable, so pathetic, that they could have started an international incident. That is, if they could have started.

For the outdoor writers Castro arranged for each of their boats to be powered by an outboard motor called the Mockba. He'd gotten this great deal from the Soviet Union, where they were manufactured. Apparently, Castro never heard of the Mockba's worldwide reputation—as the worst outboard motor ever made by mankind.

If Castro was fishing for compliments from the outdoor writers after their 1978 trip, he came away empty-handed. Their Cold War attitudes were still chilly, not only toward him but also the Soviet Union. All thanks to the Mockba. Said one writer after his Cuban excursion, "If the Russians make intercontinental ballistic missiles like they make their outboard motors, America has nothing to worry about."

Castro had invited the group to fish for bass in Lake Redonda and stay as his guests at the government-owned fishing camp. He even provided them with twelve government-owned fishing skiffs, each one powered by a government-owned Mockba.

"The first thing I noticed when we went down to the lakeshore was that none of the motors had their covers on," said Bob McNally, outdoor editor of the *Florida Times Union*. "I asked one of the guides why all the motors had their cowlings off and he explained there were two reasons. First, the motors had no shutoff arrangement, not even a choke. So the only way to stop them was to put your hand over the air intake on the carburetor. And, secondly, the motors broke down so much, there was no point in keeping the covers on, since you were always taking them off to either stop the motor or fix it."

In fact, the motors broke down so much that one of the twelve skiffs was used as a motor-repair boat. It putted around the lake with spare motors in it to replace the ones that quit. To make it easier for the Americans to get help, each boat had a little white flag attached to a pole, which the angler was to put up when he needed help. The mechanic's boat then would come over and either fix the motor on the spot, or yank it off and replace it with a new Mockba.

"Our motor broke down three times the first day and was finally replaced," recalled McNally. "But the replacement engine failed the second time the guide tried to start it.

"All day long the guides fussed with those motors. Starting it was a nightmare and stopping it was a joke. White flags kept sprouting up all over the place.

"We found out later that those twelve skiffs had used up seventy-eight new Mockbas in one year. Whatever *glasnost* brings in the future in the way of Soviet-American relations, you can bet it won't bring Mockba outboards to America."

Paul Cieslik
Lahaina, Hawaii, 1985

Australian naval seaman Paul Cieslik wanted to catch some fun on a "borrowed" fishing boat. But the only thing he caught was plenty of hell—for wrecking nineteen deep-sea fishing boats in a Hawaiian harbor.

It was an orgy of destruction that stood the island of Lahaina on its ear and had repercussions all the way back to Cieslik's native Australia.

The wild spree began at three A.M. one June morning in 1985 when Cieslik was on shore leave from his ship, the H.M.A.S. *Supply,* which was anchored off the island after participating in naval exercises. After partying on Lahaina all evening Cieslik decided to test the fishing waters. According to local authorities the twenty-three-year-old sailor broke into the charter fishing vessel *Aerial* and managed to get it started. But unfortunately for Cieslik—and soon for the rest of the boats in the harbor—the *Aerial* had a steering problem that required extensive repair.

Cieslik put the forty-four-foot boat at full throttle, shot out of the slip, immediately lost control of the boat—and blasted into the bow of the neighboring *Sea Wolf.*

The *Aerial* careened off the *Sea Wolf,* plowed into ten other boats, and finally speared the bow of the fancy deep-sea fishing boat *Waterworks.* The tremendous impact slammed the *Waterworks* into six other boats moored alongside, and damaged them too.

For the awesome Aussie the evening suddenly had become quite smashing. And he wasn't done yet.

He dived overboard, swam out to the thirty-six-foot *Broadbill,* hot-wired the boat, and tried to make a getaway. By that time police had rushed to the scene of the harbor havoc. Two officers and a couple of boat owners hopped aboard another boat and raced after the *Broadbill,* which was rapidly disappearing into a fogbank.

During the frantic high-speed chase, police said, Cieslik tried to ram his boat into theirs three different times. A Coast Guard cutter joined the chase but couldn't catch the runaway

sailor either. In the fog the pursuers got confused and ended up chasing after another boat—and Cieslik got away.

At seven A.M.—four hours after the sailor's fishing-excursion-turned-mayhem—the *Broadbill* was found grounded on a reef off the island of Lanai with her bottom and keel ripped out. Minutes later police found Cieslik hiding in a fisherman's shack on a deserted beach.

The sailor was charged with stealing two boats, unauthorized control of a propelled vehicle, criminal property damage, and attempted criminal property damage. The H.M.A.S. *Supply* sailed back to Australia without Cieslik, leaving him in jail to face a possible sentence of twenty years in prison.

The next morning the harbor looked as if a cyclone had hit it, with boats piled atop one another. Most of the damaged boats were laid up for repairs for a month. The cost of the destruction: a whopping $350,000.

After protests from Hawaiian officials, the Australian government finally picked up the tab. Those who knew Cieslik were astonished by his actions. They described the handsome young sailor as a polite, hardworking guy who'd never been in trouble before.

Two months after he was arrested, Cieslik pleaded no contest and got off without prison time. A chastened, wiser man, Cieslik said aloha to Hawaii—and Hawaii said good riddance to him.

Erbin Baumgartner

Kingsport, Tennessee, 1969

Just as every workman needs a good tool, every fisherman needs a good boat. Erbin Baumgartner decided the best way to get a good boat was to build his own . . . but the final result wasn't exactly what he'd anticipated.

Erbin, a lanky, bespectacled reporter for the Kingsport,

Tennessee, *Times-News,* hadn't really built anything big with his own hands before. But that minor fact didn't deter him.

He gathered wood, nails, caulking, and other materials in the basement of his home and—like Noah—set to work on a boat that would weather any storm.

Night after night he toiled, whistling and humming and occasionally yelping as he whacked a finger with the hammer. Slowly the boat took shape, and after several weeks it was finished. As he looked over his masterpiece, Erbin decided it was a splendid craft, wide enough so there was no chance of it capsizing.

Unfortunately, it was too wide. When he tried to take it out of the basement, he discovered the boat wouldn't fit through the lone narrow doorway! Erbin cursed and set to work removing the door frame. That did the trick. Pushing and tugging, he squeezed his boat through the doorway.

Now the boat was in his yard. Neighbors came over to inspect it. As they circled the boat, Erbin could tell by their hushed demeanor that they were suitably awed by his superb craftsmanship but doubtful that it would float.

Even when one man said, "You really gonna try to go fishin' in that thing?" Erbin wasn't bothered. Sure, the boat wasn't as sleek as a Hydra-Sport, but Erbin thought he'd done a great job.

He decided the launching of his amazing vessel shouldn't go unnoticed by the world. Such anonymity was for lesser fishing boats. His craft, a boat for the ages, deserved recognition. So he arranged for a *Times-News* photographer to record his maiden voyage for posterity.

With the photographer standing on shore, Erbin paddled his craft out into the waters of a nearby lake, grinning from ear to ear. But Erbin's grin vanished as he looked down and saw water gurgling into the boat. Something had gone horribly, horribly wrong!

Water was fast leaking into his boat. Erbin frantically sloshed water out of the boat with both hands. His craft, his pride and joy, just couldn't sink! But water gushed in faster than he could bail it out. The bow began dipping below the lake's surface.

Finally, realizing he was defeated, Erbin gave up. He turned toward the camera—and saluted as he went down with his ship. He was still holding his salute when the water reached his ears.

He'd literally gone down in the annals of boat-building history. It may have been an ignoble incident to Erbin, but it made a terrific full-page photo spread in the *Times-News*'s next edition.

Three Men and a Fish

Three jubilant Florida fishermen hauled a six-hundred-pound jewfish aboard their eighteen-foot boat—then watched in horror as the huge fish turned the tables on them by sinking the boat.

Despite small craft warnings the three had gone fishing anyway and were delighted to have caught several large grouper. Then they were overjoyed when they captured the gigantic jewfish. But their joy turned to sorrow when the huge fish overbalanced the boat and caused it to capsize.

The anglers—Jody Weiss and Bill Gaukier, both of Marco Island, and Jeff Smith, of Naples—spent more than twelve hours in rough Gulf of Mexico waters clinging to their capsized hull before being rescued by the Coast Guard.

The jewfish, meanwhile, had swum away.

Loni Anderson's Parents
White Bear Lake, Minnesota, 1956

When television beauty Loni Anderson was a child, her parents wanted to teach her the joys of fishing. But what started out as a fun day turned into a black comedy.

Loni, who starred on *WKRP in Cincinnati,* was ten years old when her parents, Klayton and Maxine, took her for a day of fishing at White Bear Lake, a short drive from their home in

St. Paul, Minnesota. Klayton had bought a brand-new pole and planned to show Loni how to fish with it off the dock. Meanwhile, Maxine was relaxing on the family's moored pontoon boat, happily watching her husband teach their young daughter the art of catching fish.

"I was sitting on the dock with my dad when a huge fish came along, hit the hook, and then took off with Dad's new pole," recalled Loni. "Dad wasn't about to lose that pole, so he climbed into our pontoon boat and took off after the fish and the pole. My mother remained on the boat while I stayed behind on the dock."

Klayton chased after the runaway fishing pole, which was bobbing up and down as the fish furiously swam away. Halfway across the lake Klayton jumped into the water and grabbed the pole. Instead of swimming back to the boat, he treaded water and tried to reel in the fish. But the line broke and the fish got away.

"Meanwhile, my mother was hysterical," recalled Loni. "She didn't know how to drive the boat and it was going all over the lake. My dad was floating in the water yelling, 'Pick me up! Pick me up!' As I was watching all this, I knew it was dangerous—but it was so funny!"

Finally, Klayton managed to grab one of the pontoons as the boat motored by him. Before he could climb onto the deck and shut off the engine, however, the boat rammed onto the beach and smashed into a rock. Fortunately, no one was hurt, but the boat ended up in the repair shop.

"That was one of my favorite times with my mom and dad," said Loni. "It was like watching a Marx Brothers movie!"

Ken Schultz

Catskill Mountains, New York, 1982

A simple trial run of a new engine turned into a mortifying, wet, and cold experience for *Field and Stream* fishing editor Ken Schultz.

"Two days before the opening of trout season I had finished rigging a new boat and got everything in fishing order," Schultz said. "Meanwhile, my family and I had been graciously invited by Jewish neighbors to attend a Passover seder observance in their home at three o'clock that afternoon. I finished work on the boat in the morning and left at one o'clock to test my brand-new motor on the lake."

Schultz told his wife he'd be back in plenty of time to make the three o'clock observance. After all, he was only going to a lake in the Catskills not far from their home to give the engine a quick trial run. He wasn't going fishing or anything. He promised he'd be there on time, assuring his wife there was no way he would be late.

Oh, yeah?

A steady galelike wind whistled across the shallow lake when Schultz launched the boat, but he wasn't concerned. He started up the engine and it turned right over. However, whenever he tried to put the boat into forward or reverse, the engine stalled. That was frustrating. After ten minutes it wouldn't start at all. That was downright disconcerting.

By now, the wind had pushed Schultz three hundred yards farther out in the lake. Of course, he still had his electric trolling motor, which he quickly pressed into action. But the wind was too strong for such a small motor and he couldn't make any headway at all. Worse, there wasn't another boat on the lake, so he couldn't hope for any help from a passerby.

Schultz assessed the situation. It was March, the water was thirty-nine degrees, he was wearing a snowmobile suit, and he had a promise to keep. He had only one option left. Schultz jumped overboard in the knee-to-chest-high water and walked the boat. He didn't actually walk. Rather he slowly sloshed and stumbled his way to the shore for "what seemed like an eternity."

101

A shivering, wet Schultz finally reached the ramp, winched the boat onto his trailer, and, still clad in his soggy outfit, sped off to his neighbor's house.

"I was thirty minutes late, wet from perspiration and water, still in my snowmobile suit, feet frozen, and looking like a wild-eyed fisherman," Schultz recalled. "My wife wouldn't speak to me. My kids were asking loudly where I'd been, and the host and other guests, neatly attired and clutching wine-glasses, stared at me like I was some kind of nut."

Schultz's trial run was aptly named. What started out as a pleasant day for him turned into a real trial.

Lieutenant Governor Bobby Brantley

Lake Jackson, Florida, 1989

Florida Lieutenant Governor Bobby Brantley proudly launched his brand-new twenty-thousand-dollar Ranger bass boat—and almost sank his reputation as a brainy fisherman.

"I had been fishing for a number of years, but mostly out of small, nondescript boats," recalled Brantley. But, as his political career prospered, he finally achieved the dream of so many bass fishermen—he bought a top-of-the-line Ranger.

"It was the first really fancy boat I had ever owned. I knew I was going to really impress the guys at the boat ramp."

The very first Saturday after picking up the boat, he and a friend headed for the ramp at Tallahassee's Lake Jackson and got into the launch line. Brantley stepped out of his truck, proud as a peacock over his new toy, and undid the retaining straps of the boat. When he got it all ready to launch, he climbed in.

"My partner backed the boat down to the water and it floated right off the trailer," Brantley recalled. "Everything was going just fine. He pulled the truck and trailer up to find a parking spot and I just waited for him."

While he waited, Brantley was showing off his new boat. Just then the first sign of trouble arose. His bilge pump started spewing lots of water out the side of the boat. Then the boat began settling lower and lower in the water.

"I looked around trying to figure out what I had done wrong," he said. "I mean, everything had been going so well, the boat looked so beautiful. Then it suddenly occurred to me . . . I forgot to put the plug in!

"It happens sooner or later to everybody, I guess, but why me? And why then? All those guys sitting around in their little fourteen-foot johnboats started laughing at me in my twenty-thousand-dollar Ranger that was slowly sinking under me."

Brantley jumped up on the bow and started yelling and whistling for his partner to come back with the trailer before the boat completely filled up with water and sank. Fortunately, Brantley and his partner managed to save the boat just in the nick of time.

"Everybody at the Lake Jackson ramp was laughing and applauding as my partner pulled me back out," said Brantley. "I guess I didn't impress them with my new boat as much as I thought I would."

SWALLOWING THE BAIT

The Silliest Fishing Pranks

Ted Kelly

Lake Seminole, Georgia, 1983

No guide had a more shameless sense of humor than Ted Kelly.

Like an angler toying with a doomed fish Ted played mind games with bass pro Penny Berryman. His exaggerations of the dangers lurking in a lake had Penny nearly frozen with fright—and wrecked any chance she had of doing well in an upcoming bass tournament.

Penny, one of the all-time leading money winners on the Bass'n Gal tour, wanted to scout Lake Seminole a few weeks before the tourney was to get under way there. Since she hailed from Arkansas and had never fished this particular lake before, she hired Ted Kelly as her guide. Penny had no idea what she was letting herself in for when she asked him to show her his favorite fishing spot.

Ted and Penny hopped into her boat and he told her to head toward a line of cypress trees in the distance. "We entered this incredibly narrow, spooky waterway in the line of trees," Penny recalled. "It was like a tunnel, with a canopy of vegetation overhead. And it was real dark."

It was here that the Georgia guide decided to have a little fun at Penny's expense. "I gotta warn ya, it's real shallow in here, so watch out for obstructions," Ted drawled.

Suddenly, the water exploded just ahead and off to one side of the boat. Penny's heart jumped into her throat. She looked just in time to see a huge alligator slap his tail on the surface and glare at them. Up to that time Penny had never seen an alligator except in Tarzan movies.

"Oh, yeah, I gotta warn ya," said Ted. "Some of the obstructions in here are gators. There're lots of 'em."

As Penny's eyes adjusted to the darkness, she peered around and realized that there were alligators everywhere. A chill slithered up her spine, especially when Ted started greeting the gators, calling each one by name, as though they were old friends.

As Penny slowly and cautiously moved the boat ahead, wondering what she had gotten herself into, Ted pointed to some low-hanging vines ahead and said, "Oh, and another thing. See those vines? I gotta warn ya, they're called cow itch. There're lots of 'em in here. Don't let 'em touch ya. If ya let 'em touch ya, they'll burn a hole in your skin right to the bone."

Finally, to Penny's relief, they came to the end of the cypress tunnel that opened out into a little circular pond surrounded by cypress stumps. Ted told her this area of Lake Seminole was called Red Lake and that it held some big bass. He recommended that she cast her lure right up next to the cypress stumps. Happy that she could now concentrate on the fish instead of on any more "dangers," Penny was set to make her first cast when Ted cleared his throat.

"Oh, and another thing," he told her. "I gotta warn ya. Be real careful ya don't actually hit any of those stumps with your lure. There're wasps' nests in those stumps—two-inch-long red wasps. And if ya disturb 'em, they'll fly up your fishing line and attack ya. And the only way ya can get away from 'em is to jump in the water."

Penny didn't dare get close to the stumps.

A few minutes later, after thunder rumbled in the far distance, Ted pointed to a number of dead trees encircling the small lake. They appeared to have been burned. "Oh, yeah, I forgot to warn ya," he said. "See all those trees? They've all been hit by lightning. This place attracts lightning like a magnet. Never come here if there're any rain clouds around."

By now Penny was a wreck and she hardly caught a thing the rest of the day. Needless to say, she didn't go near Red Lake a few weeks later when she fished the tournament. As a result she fished where the fish weren't biting and finished out of the money.

"I vowed I would never go back there again," said Penny. But later, when she learned that Ted had been pulling her leg, she returned to fish the Red Lake area once more. Without having to worry about the lake's dangers, she did great. "I won eighteen thousand dollars," said Penny. "And it was my first national-fishing-tournament victory."

Bobby Wilkes

Lake Oklawaha, Florida, 1978

The zaniest catch that angler Bobby Wilkes ever netted was the star in a prank that scared a fellow fisherman right out of his boots.

Wilkes, who once owned the JW Lure Company, was fishing in a small club tournament on Florida's Lake Oklawaha off the St. Johns River near the town of Welaka.

Fishing was really lousy that day because a cold front had moved in, making the fish too sluggish to bite. Wilkes and his partner had flailed away with every lure they owned and scored a big fat zero. Apparently, so had everyone else on the lake.

As the day wore on and the fishing continued to stink, Wilkes looked for a way to amuse himself. His eyes fell on a flock of coots, ducklike water birds that gather on lakes in large numbers. Usually, whenever a boat approaches the coots, they take off just in time. But not always.

So Wilkes, who was bored with fishing, decided to make a sport of catching a coot. Stationed at the front of the boat, Wilkes started swatting at the coots with a landing net. Eventually, he netted one of the birds and quickly dumped it into the live well, where it was kept all day.

When Wilkes finally returned to the ramp, a dozen club members were standing around, grumbling about the rotten day. One of the anglers asked Wilkes how he'd done.

"Well, it wasn't much," said Wilkes, "but we did get one—about eight pounds."

"Oh, yeah? The heck you did," retorted the fisherman.

"I really do have one about eight pounds," insisted Wilkes. "It's in the live well."

"No way," snapped the man. "I've got to see this." And with that said he walked over to Wilkes's boat, bent over the live well, and opened it.

Out flew an angry black coot, right into the face of the startled and now terrified angler. The bird beat a tattoo on the fisherman's face and then flew off. It left a flock of feathers floating around in its wake . . . a group of anglers laughing themselves silly . . . and one very shaken fisherman trying to catch his breath.

John Heslep

Sinking Creek, Virginia, 1973

Veteran Virginia wildlife officer John Heslep got his man . . . and wound up feeling like a fool.

On the first day of April in 1973 Heslep was patrolling in Craig County when he received a call on his radio from the sheriff's department that someone was fishing on the bank of the Sinking Creek, one of the county's best trout streams. Since the opening of the trout season was still a week away, Heslep, along with an auxiliary officer named Zeke, sped over to the creek.

When they arrived at a spot near where the angler was reported to be fishing, Heslep left Zeke with the car to block any escape by land. Heslep then took a hand-held radio with him as he walked along a ridge overlooking the creek.

Soon he spotted the culprit boldly fishing on the bank near an International Scout four-wheel drive. Heslep carefully studied the situation and planned to stalk his prey. A misty rain was falling as he quietly crept down the ridge and into a tree line that masked his approach for part of the quarter mile he had to negotiate.

As Heslep glided cautiously through the trees, he avoided stepping on any loose branches and congratulated himself for his Indian-like stealth. Stopping at the edge of the trees, he surveyed what lay ahead—a newly plowed field stretching about 125 yards.

Heslep moved into a crouch and started across the field . . . and sank in mud up to his waist. Undaunted, he tried to quietly unstick himself. Apparently, the squish he made as he emerged from the mud went unnoticed as his quarry continued to fish. The officer was glad that the angler—clad in a bright plaid shirt, new overalls, and leather boots—seemed so focused on fishing that he hadn't noticed someone creeping up behind him.

Soon Heslep was crawling on his hands and knees. By the time he made it to the Scout, his uniform was soaked from the rain and the mud. But he didn't care—he was too pleased with his sneaky, quiet approach.

"I thought I'd really done something great, getting that close to him without him hearing me," recalled Heslep. The officer then crept forward from the Scout and got within a foot of the man. "And he still didn't hear me."

Finally Heslep cleared his throat and said, "You're kind of rushing the season a little, aren't you?"

There was no reaction.

The puzzled officer then walked in front of the man to confront him—and got the shock of his life. That was no fisherman. It was a carefully constructed stuffed dummy!

The chagrined Heslep radioed his partner, "Hey, Zeke, I've got some kind of dummy down here."

"It would take a dummy to fish in this kind of weather," replied Zeke.

"No, Zeke, I mean a real dummy—a dummy dummy." Heslep still couldn't figure out what was going on. So he reeled in the line on the rod that had been placed in the dummy's hands. The officer then shook his head and laughed when he saw what was at the end of the hook—a cardboard fish with the words *April Fool!*

"That's when I realized what day it was," Heslep recalled.

Later, the bamboozled officer learned that three local teenagers whom he knew had driven to the creek in the Scout, set up the dummy, and called the sheriff's department to report an illegal fisherman. Then the boys watched Heslep's whole half-hour stalk from the other side of the creek while they snickered their heads off.

Heslep took the prank good-naturedly; he didn't even impound their vehicle. But after the officer left and the boys came out of hiding to hop into the Scout, they found someone had mysteriously let all the air out of the tires.

April Fool.

Something Fishy Is Going on Down There

Former ambassador, editor, and congresswoman Clare Boothe Luce nearly drove an innocent fisherman crazy.

"I've never forgotten that zany episode," said Luce. "I was scuba-diving in the tropics and falling in love with bright, beautiful, interesting fish when I suddenly saw an enormous baited fish-hook. I looked up and saw a boat above me. I don't know what got into me, but I grabbed the bait off the hook and gave it to the fish.

"Right away the hook was yanked up—and then it came down with another bait. I took the bait again, and he yanked again. We went back and forth like this until I finally grabbed the line above the hook and allowed myself to be reeled right up beside the boat.

"That man was the most surprised fisherman you ever saw!"

Tom McNally

Alligator Alley, Florida, 1961

So how does a tarpon get from one side of the road to the other? It walks, or rather flips and flops, across. At least that's what Tom McNally had a carload of tourists from New York believing.

McNally is the former outdoor editor of the *Chicago Tribune* and one of America's most famous outdoor writers. One day in 1961 he was fly-casting along Alligator Alley, a Florida highway that cuts across the Everglades in a straight line from Fort Lauderdale to the west coast of the state. A deep canal borders each side of the road.

McNally was bank-fishing alongside the road and scoring regularly on baby tarpon, most of them just five pounds or so. Suddenly, he hooked a twenty-pound-plus tarpon. A tarpon that size on a fly rod can really tear up some water, and this one put on a spectacular show. It raced up and down the canal, jumped several times, and finally headed straight for the bank that McNally was standing on.

With a magnificent effort the tarpon leapt from the canal, barely touching the bank, and spit out McNally's fly. Then it flipped right onto Alligator Alley. From there it proceeded to flip, flop, and jump its way across the highway, down the bank on the other side—and right into the canal across the way!

During the tarpon's acrobatics a car with New York license plates came screeching to a halt on the Alley and several excited adults and children piled out. They watched in amazement as the tarpon flopped its way across the highway right in front of their car.

"What the heck was that?" asked one of the New Yorkers.

"Beats me," said another. "I've never seen anything like that before."

They stood in silent awe at the edge of the road and peered down at the canal in which the fish had finally plopped. When McNally, with fly rod in hand, ambled up to them, the tourists surrounded the angler like gnats.

"Mister, do you know what that was?" asked one of them.

113

McNally saw a golden opportunity for a little fun. He just couldn't resist pulling the wool over the city slickers' eyes.

"Oh, that happens all the time," he said with a straight face. "That was a tarpon, and whenever one of them wants to go from the canal on one side of the road to the canal on the other side, it just jumps across."

The duly impressed tourists shook their heads in wonder. As they piled back into their car, McNally heard one of them say, "Wait'll we tell the folks back home about this!"

Bing McClellan's "Friends"

Michigan City, Indiana, 1967

With a little help from his "friends" Bing McClellan put on an exhibition of long-distance casting that sent him reeling in embarrassment.

It all happened back when coho salmon were first stocked into the Great Lakes and every city along the shoreline was trying to become the "Coho Capital of the World." McClellan, owner of Burke's Lures, was a well-known angler who was asked by the town of Michigan City, Indiana, to appear on a live televised seminar as part of a coho campaign.

The city held the TV show in a local football stadium attended by hundreds of spectators. They listened intently to local experts down on the field explain the tricks and tactics needed to catch salmon.

McClellan was chosen to give a demonstration of long-range casting. He waited patiently for his appearance before the crowd and the cameras. He was proud of his long-distance casting rod, which was rigged up with a heavy plug that he could sail a long way.

But unknown to McClellan, some of his friends had

briefly stolen his rod and reel and sabotaged it as a prank. Then they returned it and waited for the fun to begin.

When it was McClellan's turn on camera, he dutifully began his lecture, explaining the ins and outs of long-distance casts, and how to execute them. Then it was time for the big moment—to show the audience a long cast. He hauled back on the rod and let that sucker fly.

And fly that plug did . . . over the crowd . . . over the stands . . . and out of sight! "It must have landed a quarter a mile away," McClellan recalled.

What his friends had done was cut the line about fifteen yards down on the reel spool. That way, when he cast, the lure flew off the cut line and just kept going, and going, and going, since there was nothing holding it back.

"There I was, standing in front of hundreds of people, with a lureless rod in my hands," McClellan said. "My friends [behind the camera] were just laughing their fool heads off. I just stood there looking pretty silly, while the crowd wondered what the hell had happened.

"I never did find that plug.

"Finally, I just turned to the crowd and said, 'That's probably the longest cast you'll ever see on camera,' and then I got off the stage as fast as I could."

Archie Phillips

Apalachicola, Florida, 1962

For Archie Phillips the fibbing was just as good as the fishing.

With one trumped-up story, Archie sent an armada of fellow anglers on a trip to futility—just so he could have a fishing hole all to himself.

Archie and his son, Archie Junior, were on a fall fishing excursion to Apalachicola Bay in the Florida panhandle for saltwater trout. But the fishing was so dismal, they couldn't even have caught a cold. They didn't even get so much as a nibble during the first two days of the trip. It was the same for other anglers who were staying at the same fishing camp.

On the third day the story hadn't changed: no bites. By midmorning father and son were so discouraged that they called it quits and headed back for the marina. But with a flicker of optimism that had not yet died out, Archie Junior left a stingray grub lure trailing over the back of the boat about thirty yards behind.

Then it happened. As they approached the marina . . . BAM! . . . Archie Junior got a strike and reeled in a nice four-pound trout. Buoyed by his son's success Archie quickly tossed out a lure and, just as quickly, snared a trout too.

They laughed at the irony. They had been all over the bay. Yet there they were—within a hundred yards of the marina—finally catching trout. They netted one right after the other. By noon they had hauled in fifty nice trout, all three to five pounds.

The happy anglers then took a break for lunch back at the camp. As more and more unsuccessful fishermen arrived, word spread of the Phillipses' bonanza catch. They were soon under siege. "Where did you get those fish?" was the question of the day.

Archie pondered for a moment. He could be a great guy and share the secret of his good fishing fortune with the others. After all, wouldn't they have done the same thing for him? Wouldn't he feel bad if he didn't reveal the location of the mother lode? Archie knew exactly what he should say: "Marker 18."

Marker 18 was about eight miles out in the bay! Archie wanted his fellow fishermen as far away as possible from his spot.

The next morning Archie and his son got up late and found the camp emptied of fishermen. No doubt they were following Archie's "directions." Meanwhile, the duo leisurely motored out a hundred yards from the marina and, once again, loaded their boat with hefty trout. They had reached their limit by nine thirty in the morning.

So they took a run out to Marker 18—and found at least forty boats working the vicinity . . . all fishless. That night back at the camp, Archie was again the center of attention. "How could you catch all those fish when we were skunked?" they asked him. Archie looked them right in the eye and said he and his son had risen extra early and were out at Marker 18 three hours before daylight.

"We caught all our fish before the sun came up and then they stopped biting," he explained with a straight face.

Archie and his son went home the next morning, so he never had to face all those sleepy anglers who got up shortly after midnight the next day, hoping to catch those elusive trout at Marker 18 . . . and were left wondering why the fish there seemed to bite for Archie Phillips and his son but no one else.

Flying in the Face of Absurdity

One day in the 1940s a young Englishman approached the counter of the famed New York City fly fishing shop, the Angler's Roost, and asked about buying a dozen flies for a weekend trip.

"I can tell from that accent that you're from across the pond," proprietor Jim Deren replied. Knowing that the British tend to use small flies, he continued, "Well, mister, we use small flies here too." Deren then reached under the counter and brought up a cupped hand. "Have you ever used flies this small?"

The Englishman looked into Deren's hand—and didn't see anything. That's because there was nothing.

"Well, they're pretty small," admitted the Englishman, "but no smaller, old sport, than the ones I use." Then he put his hand in his pocket, pulled it out, and opened his palm, which was equally empty.

THE CATCH
OF THE
DAZED

The Wackiest
Things Ever
Reeled In

Fredda Lee
Lake Patoka, Indiana, 1987

Pro bass angler Fredda Lee came face-to-face with her most startling catch—and was absolutely mortified.

Fredda was fishing a small lake in Indiana on a practice day before a tournament. Although she was by herself, there were plenty of other boats nearby.

"I was slowly moving along a shoreline and casting when I felt something funny on the end of the line," Fredda recalled. "It didn't seem like a strike and it didn't feel like a fish. But it did feel like something had just grabbed hold of the lure, so I set the hook and started reeling in."

Her rod kept bending more and more, so she kept pulling and reeling. She just couldn't imagine what she had hooked, and her curiosity was killing her. "The water was pretty clear and you could see down quite a ways, so I kept staring at the water as I brought whatever it was near the boat," Fredda recalled.

Reeling in faster and faster, Fredda finally got her first glimpse at her catch—and started screaming. It definitely was not a fish.

"I saw this face in the water," she recalled. "It was coming right up at me and I just went cold all over. I thought I had hooked a human head. It scared me to death and I started hollering to all the other boats. I really started to panic."

It looked like the ugly, wrinkled face of death. It was too horrible for words. But something compelled Fredda to keep reeling. She shuddered as the sickening head drew closer to the boat. She couldn't bear to look at it. Then she did a double take.

"I looked down again and as the face got closer, I realized that it was not a human head. It was a rubber mask! It was so realistic. It even had hair on it."

After breathing a sigh of relief that she hadn't reeled in a head, Fredda was now faced with another dilemma.

"It was too late to take back all my screaming," she said. "The other boats were heading my way." There wasn't anything Fredda could do. So, with a sheepish grin on her face, she held up the mask and yelled to everyone that she was all right.

"I may have been all right," added Fredda, "but I sure was embarrassed."

Frank Warren
Stuart, Florida, 1986

Charter boat captains Kim Phillips and Frank Warren often disputed over who had the most unusual catch. But Warren finally came up with the winner—he caught an airplane!

For a while Captain Phillips held local honors for the strangest catch when he snared a submerged compact automobile with the props of his forty-eight-foot Hatteras as he was coming into a dock in Stuart, Florida. He challenged Captain Warren to try to top that.

Warren eventually did—when he hooked a Cessna 337 that had crashed into his right outrigger-trolled bait.

Fifteen miles offshore Warren was piloting his boat, the *Gannet,* and trolling big baits, hoping for blue marlin. Suddenly, a small plane appeared overhead and began circling the boat. Then it came in low.

"At first we thought he was going to drop a load of dope on us," said mate Squeaky Kelly. "He came very close to the boat and was only six feet over the water, right over our baits. The next thing we knew, he made a belly flop right on top of the right rigger bait. We never had a bigger bite than that one."

The *Gannet* circled back and picked up the pilot, who luckily was not injured. An investigation revealed that the plane's tanks had been filled with bad fuel in the Bahamas. With a sputtering engine the pilot knew he wasn't going to make it to the Florida coast. When he spotted the charter boat, he figured that would be a good spot to ditch, since rescue would be close at hand.

Crazy Catches

One of the lures of fishing is that you never know what you might catch. For example:

• In 1976 John Bembers lost his wristwatch overboard while fishing in Lake Michigan. Three years later it turned up inside the stomach of a forty-two-pound salmon caught by Thomas Kresnak, of Grand Rapids, Michigan.

Presumably the salmon had scooped up the shiny watch, thinking it was food. Incredibly, the watch still worked!

• John Fallon, Jr., lost a pouch containing a silver pocketknife and chain, his wife's wedding ring, and his wallet while on a fishing trip near West Stockbridge, Massachusetts, in 1935.

Three years later John Gannon, fishing in the same waters, boated a three-pound pickerel—and inside were all of Fallon's items in good condition!

• Gosselin Deleus lost his glasses off the English coast in 1988 when he leaned over the side of a boat and they fell into the sea.

A month later a Belgian fisherman found a pair of glasses in the belly of a monkfish caught off the Belgian coast. Deleus read about the catch in a fishing magazine and contacted the Belgian —and got his glasses back.

• It wasn't a good day for veteran fishermen Ivan Olson and Nick Hanuschewicz, but it wasn't a bad day either—they caught one small trout . . . and a thousand-pounder.

"That's the first time I ever caught one of those. I don't know if the trout stamp will cover it," Olson joked as he looked at the "catch" he and his buddy pulled in—a thousand-pound 750 cc Kawasaki motorcycle.

The men were fishing Sixmile Creek north of Madison, Wisconsin, when they saw "just a little bit of chrome." They broke a fish stringer while hauling the motorcycle out, then called police. The cycle had been stolen from Madison a month earlier.

"Besides one little trout in a nearby stream, it was the only thing we caught all day," Olson said.

Raymond Lucas

Jamaica Bay, New York, 1988

For Raymond Lucas it was the reel of fortune.

While fishing one day, he hooked a bag containing five million dollars in negotiable bonds!

And if nobody claims the booty by the end of 1991, the money is his.

His catch of a lifetime came in 1988 at the end of a day's flounder fishing in Jamaica Bay, New York, when he noticed a blue bag bobbing in the water.

"I took a gaff and fished it out," Lucas recalled. It wasn't exactly sporting, but he didn't care, considering the result. Once he opened up the bag and looked inside, he was stunned. "I didn't know what to think," he said.

So Lucas took the package home and showed it to his neighbor, Frank LaSpisa. That's when he learned just what he had caught—five negotiable bonds from the Bank of Nigeria worth a total of $5,090,058. But, honest man that he was, Lucas, along with LaSpisa, turned the bonds over to the New York Police Department.

So whose money was it? Police tracked the blue bag to a delivery firm—but officials there denied any knowledge of the money. The bonds originated in Korea and police made inquiries there, but again no one claimed them.

So police gave Lucas a receipt for the five million dollars and he walked away with his fingers crossed. They told him that if no one claims it within three years, it's all his.

Tim DeMatteis

Flint River, Ontario, Canada, 1987

Butch DeMatteis and Ernie Johnson were fishing on the Flint River in Ontario, Canada, in 1985 when their boat capsized and they washed up on two rocks—just short of a thirty-foot waterfall.

They lost all their gear and a knapsack containing Johnson's wallet and other personal effects. But since they both felt lucky to escape with their lives, they didn't worry too much about the money and gear that they had lost.

Two years later, in the summer of 1987, Tim DeMatteis, Butch's son from Ohio, was vacationing and fishing the same remote portion of the Flint River. He was casting for trout when his lure snagged something big. At first he thought he had a strike, but as he reeled it in, it wasn't fighting as a big trout should.

Tim had hooked a knapsack. But not just any knapsack. Incredibly, it was the very same one that Ernie Johnson had lost two years earlier in the boating mishap with Tim's dad! Inside the knapsack was Johnson's wallet with $225 in cash and all his credit cards.

"When he told me what he had found, I couldn't believe it," Johnson said later. The grateful Johnson rewarded Tim with a hundred dollars and said he planned to have the recovered cash "bronzed and mounted on some kind of plaque."

Ted Dempsey

Pensacola Bay, Florida, 1989

Ted Dempsey caught his first marlin—but not before he caught his own fishing rod.

The zany incident happened in 1989 when Dempsey, Captain Doug Quigley, and Wayne Anderson were fishing aboard Quigley's thirty-one-foot Bertram, the *Short Circuit,* a week before the Pensacola Big Game Fishing Tournament. It was a shakedown trip to make sure the boat, the equipment, and the anglers were ready for the following weekend's competition.

Trolling two lures, the anglers had caught a couple of wahoo, but there had been little action for an hour or so. Suddenly, Captain Quigley spotted a marlin bill slashing through a school of small dolphin near a weed patch. Making a turn, he yelled to the crew to get ready. Sure enough, the marlin left the dolphin and smashed into one of the lures.

Unfortunately, the marlin struck the rod with the lighter fifty-pound line, rather than the rod rigged with eighty-pound test. It was especially unfortunate because the lighter rod and reel turned out to have had a faulty drag setting. So when the fish struck, it ripped the whole outfit out of the rod holder.

Quigley got a sick feeling in the pit of his stomach as he helplessly watched the six-hundred-dollar custom rod and Penn International reel fly overboard and go down and out of sight. But before anyone could say anything, the eighty-pound outfit started screaming as it, too, was struck by a blue marlin that had cleared the weed patch and started tail-walking. Anderson grabbed the outfit and handed it to Dempsey so he could fight his first big blue.

The fish ran off about 250 yards of line before Dempsey could make any headway. It was a seesaw battle, but after forty-five minutes Dempsey had reeled in enough of the line to see the leader. The angler knew that meant the fish was close to the boat and the fight was about over.

But Dempsey was wrong. At the end of the leader was not a marlin but the rod and reel that had been lost overboard! And with the fish still hooked to it!

127

Here's what had happened: When the marlin hit on the original fifty-pound line and started its run, it yanked the rod and reel into the water. By chance the fish swam past the other lure from the eighty-pound line, which then snagged the roller guide of the lighter outfit. So when Dempsey was handed the heavier outfit, he and the others on board assumed the marlin was hooked on it.

Not until Dempsey pulled up the first rod and reel did they figure out what happened. Anderson gaffed the lighter outfit, quickly untangled a crow's nest in the snagged reel, and then handed it to Dempsey with the marlin still at the other end. The heavier outfit was put away.

By this time Dempsey was complaining of muscle spasms in his arms, but, determined to land that marlin, he fought on. After another exhausting hour Dempsey brought in his first big blue—a 251-pounder—to go along with the first fishing rod he ever caught.

LICENSE
TO
SPILL

The Funniest
Cases of
Anglers
Falling Overboard

Dick Ramsey

St. Johns River, Florida, 1980

In his most embarrassing outing ever, veteran fishing guide Dick Ramsey found himself stranded on a ten-foot pole. And no one would touch him.

"I should have known it was going to be a bad day when my electric trolling motor didn't work," said Ramsey, famous for his lunker-bass catches on Florida's St. Johns River.

One day in 1980 he was hired by two relatively new anglers for some bass fishing. Ramsey ran his bass boat into the spring-fed Salt Run off the St. Johns. His strategy called for them to slip into the run and look around carefully until they spotted a big bass on a bed. Then they would stealthily cast a bait to the bass.

Normally, Ramsey would have used his trolling motor to maneuver through the area, because the five-foot-deep bottom was very soft and silty. But when they got back in there, he discovered his electric motor wouldn't work. He would have to use a push pole. "Poling the boat there is difficult because every time you plant the pole in the bottom, it sinks into the muck," said Ramsey.

He picked up his pole and began to propel the boat along the run while looking for bass. It was a windy day and Ramsey had just planted the pole for a good push when a strong gust blew the boat into the pole, shoving it deep into the bottom. He pulled up on the pole to free it at the exact moment when another wind gust suddenly swung the boat away from the pole.

"I held on to the pole, and the next thing I knew, that was all I had—the boat kicked out from under me and left me dangling on the end of the pole in the middle of Salt Run," recalled Ramsey. "My weight started to sink the pole deeper into the muck, so I climbed farther up the pole to stay out of the water."

Then the pole sank some more. So Ramsey climbed up some more. Then the pole sank some more.

"My two customers in the boat were very inexperienced and didn't even know how to run a boat," he said. "They tried to start it to come to my rescue, but they were helpless and just stood gaping at me as the boat drifted farther away. There were three or four other guides nearby—but they were all laughing too hard at me to help."

Meanwhile, the pole kept sinking and Ramsey kept climbing in a desperate effort to stay dry. Eventually, he ran out of pole and slipped quietly beneath the surface.

"The other guides were still laughing uncontrollably as I swam back to my boat," said Ramsey. "Ever since it happened, I had hoped to forget about it. But my fellow guides won't let me. They still laugh about it. I'll never live that day down."

Al Lindner
Crosby, Minnesota, 1982

About the only saving grace for a fisherman who suffers an embarrassing moment is that few, if any, people get to see it.

No such luck for Al Lindner. Millions of television viewers witnessed his plunge into shame.

It happened in 1982 when Lindner, the director of the In-Fisherman Communications Network, was signed to do a TV commercial for Berkley Trilene fishing line. The script called for Lindner to be in his boat near the shoreline. He was supposed to lean over a large tree branch and hold up a huge bass that he had just retrieved from the lake in the midst of partially submerged tree limbs and brush. He was to say, "I can't believe a line this thin can be so strong."

The shooting was staged at a small gravel pit outside Crosby, Minnesota, on a sunny but crisp fall afternoon. With the water temperature at a bone-numbing forty-two degrees, Lindner knew the last thing he wanted to do was get wet.

Everything was set—the tree branch was tested to make sure it would hold, the boat was ready, a big bass was on the line, and the background looked like a maze of downed trees. The scene looked perfect for a commercial designed to impress any fisherman with the strength of that line. It was a slick, well-planned Hollywood-type TV commercial. But nature had other ideas when the cameras started rolling.

"Action!" the director yelled. Lindner, positioned on the bow of the boat, leaned over the tree branch to yank the bass out of the water. But then something happened that was not in the script—the branch broke and Lindner went plunging into the icy water.

At first nobody said a word. They were astounded that the limb broke because it had been checked and double-checked.

Lindner finally popped to the surface and found himself looking directly at an open-mouthed director and an equally astonished cameraman. Lindner noticed that the camera was still running and told himself, *Say something, dummy.*

So the dripping wet, shivering Lindner held up the bass and gasped, "I can't believe a line this thin can be so strong."

Then he hauled himself into the boat before the water sucked all the warmth from his body.

The whole incident took only twenty seconds. The director looked at the cameraman and said, "Did you get it?" The cameraman nodded. "Then cut and wrap it up," the director said. "We can't do better than that."

And that's the way the commercial was shown on TV. "It didn't turn out the way we had planned," said Lindner. "But people say it was the best commercial I ever made. Too bad it had to be my most embarrassing moment."

Making a Splash

One day in the early 1940s *The New York Times* rod-and-gun editor Ray Camp visited an exclusive fishing club in the Catskills the day before the trout season opened.

He and a buddy went down to the stream and prowled around the bank. When Camp leaned out over a deep pool where the stream undercut the bank, his friend playfully shoved him into the icy water.

Camp took the prank in good humor. Early the next morning he went back to the same pool and found his friend leaning over the bank. Camp crept up behind him and shoved him into the water.

But when the victim surfaced in the frost-fringed pool, Camp was shocked to discover that he hadn't dunked his friend but the president of the fishing club instead!

The next day the president canceled his subscription to the *Times*.

Chuck Taylor

St. Johns River, Florida, 1975

Like any good fishing guide, Chuck Taylor loved to impress his customers with his uncanny knowledge of the local water. But one time he got a little too cocky for his own good.

Taylor, a noted bass guide on the St. Johns River in Florida, had a new client—a quiet, elderly man—whom he really wanted to please. He zipped the man down the river and over to the east shore of Lake George, where he planned to fish his favorite spot.

To reach it Taylor knew he had to pole the boat across a large sandbar to a deep trough of water on the inside, where the big fish were. "I had it down to an exact science, like a veteran river guide should," he said. "I'd run at it with the boat on full plane, and just about the time the customer figured we were going to plow into the sand bar, I'd cut the engine and hit the trim switch to bring the motor out of the water. Then I'd leap from the driver's seat, grab my push pole, bounce up to the front deck, and give the pole a couple of good strokes. The momentum of the boat would help us slide across that bar with almost no work on my part. The timing had to be perfect, but it always worked, and it looked impressive."

Except once. On this unforgettable day Taylor full-throttled the boat toward the sand bar and noticed that the elderly client's eyes were getting as big as a pair of largemouth bass. The frightened angler thought for sure that Taylor was going to run them aground. But at the last second the veteran guide cut the engine, hit the trim switch, and charged forward with the pole.

"My timing was perfect, as usual," recalled Taylor. "But what I didn't realize was that a strong south wind had blown all night and pushed some water out of the lake, dropping the water level a few very critical inches.

"As I charged to the bow with the pole, the keel of the boat met hard sand and the boat came screeching to a halt. But I didn't. I kept right on going over the bow and hit the water

135

still running. I tried to maintain my balance, but flopped face forward, spread eagled, over the bar.

"I came up coughing and spitting water, with grass hanging all over my face. I rolled over into a sitting position and looked up at the boat. And just then the old gentleman peeked over the bow of the boat, looked at me, and with the most deadpan expression I've ever seen, said, 'What's your hurry, son?'

"I don't think I impressed him."

Edna Mills
Lake Palestine, Texas, 1986

Pro bass angler Edna Mills loves to fish but is terrified of the water. She can't swim and doesn't even want to learn how, because she has no intention of getting wet. But she did fall out of her boat once during a bass tournament—and her terror left her with a mortifying moment that she will never forget.

"Water is made for fishing," said the Conroe, Texas, native. "That's what I was taught when I was growing up. We never went to the lake for swimming or anything like that. We went to the lake for fishing. I was taught respect for the water —you stayed in the boat and you fished."

But in 1986 Mills fell out of a boat the one and only time in her life—during a bass tournament on Lake Palestine. It happened moments after she and a male fishing partner had gotten their boat hung up on a submerged tree stump. Standing up in the boat, Mills tried rocking the craft to make it come free. But she lost her balance and took a header into the murky brown water.

"I was petrified," she recalled. "As soon as I hit the water, I grabbed the side of the boat and hung on for dear life. I also brought my knees up to my chin. It was a panic reflex. I knew that if I put my feet straight down and couldn't touch bottom, I'd freak out.

"As luck would have it, my partner in the boat couldn't help me. He'd just had back surgery and couldn't lift anything. He just sat there giving me advice as I clung to the boat.

"If you've ever tried to climb back into a boat with your knees tucked up under your chin, you know how hard it is. But I finally managed to pull myself aboard after about ten minutes of struggling. I must have looked a sight trying to maneuver myself aboard.

"When I plopped down on the deck of the boat, I was exhausted and gasping for breath. I shuddered to think how close I could have come to drowning. Then I glanced at my depth finder. I'm five feet eight inches tall—and my depth finder read only four feet! I could have stood up on the lake bottom and easily climbed back into the boat!"

John Torian
Toledo Bend Lake, Texas, 1980

John Torian made one of the most odds-defying, embarrassing plunges ever by a guide.

Before he became a tournament angler, Torian, like most pro bass fishermen, used to earn his living as a fishing guide. He often worked on Toledo Bend Lake in Texas, which was noted for its stumps and underwater logs. It's a lake that can humble the most experienced of guides, because the boat can hit a hidden stump or log and pitch the unwary fisherman into the drink.

"I've done it, and so has every other guide," Torian said. But he still has trouble believing what happened to him one day in 1980, when he was guiding a client who had been out with him a year earlier. "I remembered him well," said Torian. "He was from Iowa, but with as many customers as a guide has, you don't always remember the exact details of every trip. But obviously he did."

On this day Torian got his bait hung up on a stump and as he leaned over to clear it, he put the trolling motor in reverse. He was squatting down to pull the lure free when the boat hit a stump behind him. "I went right off the deck and did a back flip into the water," he recalled. "It was smooth and fluid. In fact, I even had time to lay my rod down on the deck as I was flipping over.

"When I climbed back into the boat, I saw my customer looking at me kind of funny. He wasn't laughing, he just had this strange look on his face. Finally he asked, 'Do you do this with every customer?' I asked him what he meant by that and he replied, 'I don't know if you remember this or not, but when I was out with you last year, you did the exact same thing.'

"I was stunned. I mean, I was guiding two hundred to two hundred fifty days a year then and I fell out of the boat maybe once a year. I couldn't believe that I fell out of the boat in front of the same customer two years in a row. But I did."

Shaw Grigsby

Lake Kissimmee, Florida, 1978

When pro angler Shaw Grigsby started his tournament career, he wanted the veterans to take notice that he belonged on the same water with them.

They took notice, all right—that he belonged *in* the same water *without* them.

In one of his first professional tournaments at Lake Kissimmee, Florida, Grigsby had drawn a well-known fisherman, Ray Tester, as his partner. The rookie wanted to make a good impression and act professionally, yet he still had his own way of fishing.

"In those days I used to take my shoes off when I was in the boat," recalled Grigsby, a winner of the Red Man All-American. "I'd keep the shoes in a dry place, and I enjoyed the comfort of bare feet."

Shortly after Grigsby and Tester started fishing, it began to rain. But that didn't stop the anglers from fishing. Soon, while fishing a patch of very thick reeds, Tester hooked a big bass. The anglers knew it was a large fish because they could see it wallowing around at the top of the water. But it wrapped the line around the reeds, so Tester used the trolling motor to move the boat to the fish.

"I wanted to help, so I grabbed the landing net and charged forward to give him a hand with the fish," Grigsby recalled. "Well, the rain had made that deck real slick and my bare feet had no traction. And when I ran forward, I just kept going. "I did a beautiful one-and-a-half gainer off the front deck.

"First I had to wait for Ray to stop laughing, then I handed him the net, climbed back into the boat, and netted his fish. I never felt more like a rookie."

Larry Lazoen

Port Charlotte, Florida, 1983

Fishing novices learn to do what Larry Lazoen says, not what he does.

In 1983, a Port Charlotte, Florida, cultural arts center and a local vocational college offered a fishing course aimed at retirees who had recently moved into the area. Lazoen, a veteran guide and pro tournament angler, offered to teach the course. He gave his elderly students both classroom time and actual experience in a variety of Florida fishing techniques.

One memorable day Lazoen took the class outside to a nearby canal, which had a cement fishing pier that extended out over the water. Lazoen wanted to demonstrate for his students how to rig and fish for bass with a plastic worm.

"After I had done the rigging part and made a few casts, I began to explain one of the most important aspects of worm fishing—the hook set," Lazoen said. "With a Texas-rigged plastic worm you must first drive the hook through the worm and then into the fish. It takes a forceful hook set.

"I had one gentleman attempt to set the hook a few times to illustrate the form, but he was setting the hook much too softly. I looked at him, then at the rest of the class, and explained that his soft hook set just wasn't going to do the job. So I told the class, 'I'll show you how to do it.' I then made a cast and said, 'Okay, I have a bite. Now watch this.' "

Lazoen expertly snapped the rod up with authority, took a step backward to really drive it in—and stepped right off the pier! "I went in all the way and left nothing but my hat floating on the surface," he recalled.

When Lazoen resurfaced and spit out water, he looked up at the thirty students standing on the pier and wondered what he should say. "As it turned out, one old fellow said it all. He stared down at me and said, 'If that's the way you have to set the hook, I'm not fishing.' "

Class was dismissed.

Guy Eaker

Wylie Lake, North Carolina, 1981

Some fishermen have fallen out of boats and others have slipped off bridges. But Guy Eaker managed to do both—at the same time.

It happened when Eaker, a seven-time B.A.S.S. Masters Classic qualifier, was fishing for fun with a buddy on North Carolina's Wylie Lake.

"It was nighttime in early spring and we were fishing for crappie and white bass," Eaker recalled. "The weather was still cold, so I decided to go back to the truck and get some extra jackets."

The only problem was that Eaker didn't want to move the boat. They had tied it to a bridge next to the boat ramp and then suspended lanterns from the bridge so the light would attract baitfish. The strategy was working, because they were catching fish, and Eaker was afraid that the fish would be spooked if he motored or paddled the boat to shore.

Shivering in the night chill, Eaker pondered how to get himself back to the shore without moving the boat. Then he noticed a water pipe running along the underside of the bridge. "The pipe wasn't very thick and I figured I could just kind of reach up and grab it and 'hand-walk' myself along it back to shore," he said. "Heck, I'd done that sort of hand-over-hand stuff all my life.

"So I told my buddy, Pete Heanfer, that I'd be back in a jiffy with the jackets. I reached for the pipe, but I couldn't quite touch it. So I decided to jump up and grab it, because it was only a jump of about four inches."

When Eaker jumped, he kicked the boat out from under himself. Unfortunately, he didn't jump high enough and his hands slipped off the pipe. Eaker fell straight down, only the boat wasn't underneath him anymore. He plunged right into the frigid water with a big splash.

"That water was really cold, and Pete later told me he'd never seen anybody go into the water and come out as fast as I did," said Eaker. "But now I was not only cold, I was wet and cold. So I tried it again, and this time I caught the pipe and went hand over hand back to shore."

When he reached his truck, the soaked angler faced one more indignity. He had to strip off all his wet clothes, hop inside the truck, put the heater on full blast, lay his clothes out on the seat, and sit there in the nude for two hours waiting for the clothes to dry.

"Fortunately no one came by," he said. "I think I would have had a heckuva time explaining what I was doing sitting in a truck at three in the morning naked as a jaybird."

That wasn't the only time Eaker was drenched in shame.

In 1986, he and several other pros had gathered to shoot a commercial for Stratos Boats on Percy Priest Lake in Tennessee. It was a big production with several boats.

They spent the morning doing general fishing and boating shots. In the afternoon the boats were brought together for close-ups. The director wanted to get a tight shot of Eaker standing up in the bow of his boat fishing and talking.

"We discussed the shot and how we wanted it set up, and then got the boats positioned just right for the light," Eaker recalled. "The director told me to step over into his boat so he could get my clothes arranged just the way he wanted them for the shot. I had all my fancy tournament clothes on, with sponsor patches and all. I even had a new clean hat on.

"We pulled the boats together and I went to step into the director's boat—only, I didn't make it. As I took my step, the boats parted and I went straight into the water and completely out of sight. All that was left was my new hat . . . floating peacefully on the surface.

"I came up sputtering and everybody was laughing—and I mean everybody. The cameramen, the other pros, the director. When I went back to the dock to get a change of clothes, I could still hear them all laughing.

"After we finally got the shots done, I had this horrible thought and I asked the director if he had the camera running when I took my dive. He got this real disappointed look on his face and told me he hadn't. Then he said it was one of the dumbest things he had ever done—not getting that on film.

"Well, I was glad he didn't. That was embarrassing enough without the whole world getting to see it."

Johnnie Borden

Truman Lake, Missouri, 1984

Pro bass angler Johnnie Borden has amazed his fellow fishermen with the unique way he operates his boat—he stands in the back and steers with his feet.

It looks perilous, but Borden always took pride in never having fallen out . . . until one memorable tournament.

"I use an electric trolling motor that is a hand-controlled model with an extension bracket attached to it so I can steer it with my foot," Borden explained. "Several buttons on the boat deck turn the power on and off.

"When I am fishing, I stand on one foot for balance, and use the other foot to continually move between the extension bracket and the deck buttons to control the boat. It looks a bit awkward, but I think it's the easiest way to have precise control over the boat."

And such control was exactly what Borden needed during a fishing tournament on Truman Lake in Missouri, because the lake was loaded with underwater stumps.

On the last day of the event Borden, who was in the top five on the leader board, tried using the flipping technique in the middle of a stumpy area.

"I had drawn a new partner for that day and we had fished most of the morning," Borden recalled. "I noticed he kept staring at me every now and again. Finally, he looked at me, shook his head, and said that he didn't know how I could balance there on one foot, fish, constantly bounce off the stumps, and set the hook on the fish—all without falling over the side.

"Heck, I'd been fishing that way for years and never once fallen out of the boat. I had just turned my head toward him to make some smart remark like 'Real pros never fall out of the boat,' when I got a strike. I leaned back to set the hook, and at the same time the boat hit a stump. I went right out of the boat. Backwards. All the way under!"

But Borden not only hung on to the rod, he had hooked the fish, which was now thrashing on the other side of the boat. Since the water was only three feet deep, Borden forgot about his own embarrassment and scrambled after the bass. Then he discovered that his line was wrapped around the trolling motor.

"It was a mess. There I was, dripping wet, with my rod in one hand, and trying to grab the fish with my other hand. I finally got the fish and then climbed back into the boat with my pride pretty well drenched.

"My partner was kind enough to wait until I was safely back in with the fish before he started laughing his head off."

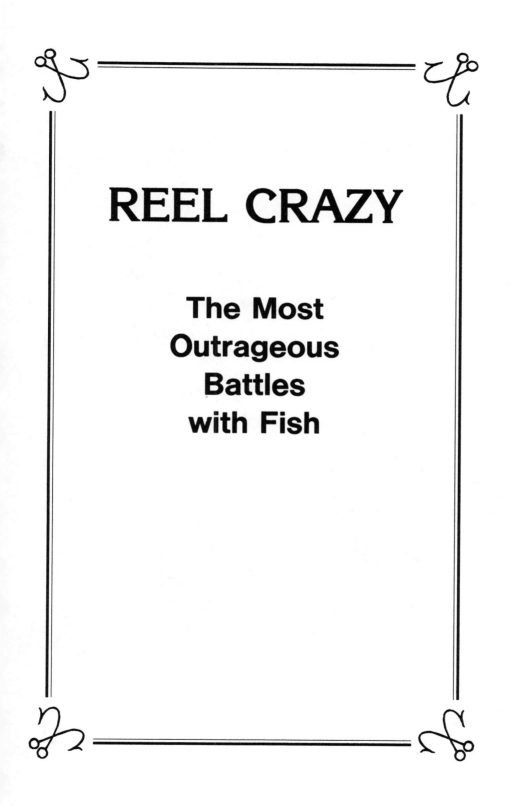

REEL CRAZY

The Most
Outrageous
Battles
with Fish

Paul Clause
Kona Coast, Hawaii, 1984

Fisherman Paul Clause thought he had snared a blue marlin. But it turned out that the fish had hooked the fisherman.

Clause, of Fairbanks, Alaska, was enjoying a vacation in Hawaii, where he had hired Captain Glenn Van Valin and his boat *Karma* to help him look for Pacific blue marlin off the Kona coast.

It was one of those bright, blue Hawaiian days when the seas are as flat as flapjacks, so it didn't take long for the zigzagging spread of smoking lures to connect with one big enough to tell the folks back home about.

For more than two long but exhilarating hours Clause fought the spirited marlin before bringing it close to the boat. Figuring the fish was all but exhausted, Van Valin climbed down from the bridge and grabbed a gaff.

Meanwhile, Clause, who was still harnessed to the fighting chair, had locked the drag on the reel. But suddenly, the marlin took off like a torpedo and then headed straight down, dragging with it not only the rod and reel but the hapless angler as well!

Incredibly, the fish had dived with such speed and strength that it had yanked the chair right off the hatch cover to which it had been bolted. Van Valin, who was leaning over the side ready to gaff the fish, turned around just in time to see the shackled Clause and his chair flying through the air. Van Valin made a desperate but futile attempt to grab Clause before the angler and the chair sailed into the water.

As the marlin dragged him deeper and deeper, Clause tried frantically to free himself from the chair. Not until he was about fifty feet below the surface did he manage to unfasten the harness and swim back to the surface, where he passed out.

After Clause was rescued and revived, he mumbled to the captain, "Now I know how a fish feels when it's hooked."

Joe Barnes and
Pete Ryan

St. Lucie River, Florida, 1957

Joe Barnes and Pete Ryan—both Midwestern muskie fishermen—were sure they knew all there was to know about handling big fish. But when it came to reeling in a tarpon, the men discovered they were all wet.

The pair had gone on vacation to a fish camp on the St. Lucie River on Florida's east coast. They couldn't wait to hook the notorious fighting tarpon that plied the river. When the camp owner warned the two out-of-staters about the tarpon's power and strength, Barnes and Ryan just scoffed at him. "Don't worry, we're longtime muskie fishermen," said Barnes. "We know how to handle big fish. There's nothing in this river that we can't deal with."

Nonetheless, the camp owner persisted. "Whatever you do," he warned, "don't bring a tarpon into the boat with you. A fish like that can tear up a boat."

The two paid scant attention to him as they hopped into a rented wooden skiff and took off down the St. Lucie. The boat was a popular model back then and built in such a way that the seats reinforced the sides.

It wasn't long before Barnes hooked the first fish, an undersized snook that put up a mild battle that did little to impress the two anglers. Like many muskie fishermen Barnes and Ryan believed that muskies were king and all other fish were inferior. And the duo were even more convinced after boating two more small fish. But still no tarpon.

Finally, Ryan hooked a tarpon—not a giant one, but a decent eighty-pounder. Fifteen minutes later Ryan was still fighting the fish, and both anglers were mildly impressed with the tarpon's aerial show and its strength. But they figured the fish had to be tiring because, to them, fifteen minutes was a long battle.

Eventually, Ryan brought the fish near the boat. But then they discovered they had no gaff. So they tried to rock the skiff, hoping they could roll the tarpon into the boat. But that didn't work; they kept taking in water over the side.

Barnes decided to take matters into his own hands. He reached into the water, grabbed the tarpon by the gill plates, and, with a mighty yank, jerked the fish over the side of the boat and onto the deck. The tarpon laid there stunned as Barnes and Ryan looked at it admiringly and congratulated each other on their teamwork.

But then the tarpon came back to life—with a vengeance. It began thrashing wildly about, first knocking a tackle box up in the air, then a water jug, then an ice chest. Ryan flung himself on top of the fish, but he was quickly bucked off like a rodeo rider dumped by a bronco. Barnes then began beating on the tarpon with the butt of the rod, but that only made the fish wilder.

With debris flying everywhere Barnes and Ryan decided the wisest course of action was to retreat to the bow of the boat and just watch. "When he tires out, we'll take him," Barnes confidently predicted.

The tarpon's powerful tail then smashed to pieces the boat's center seat—the one that played a major role in holding the boat together. With the seat gone, and the tarpon still delivering one mighty blow after another to the wooden sides, it took only a few seconds for the inevitable to happen—the boat split completely apart.

All the rods, reels, tackle, ice chests, and the rest of their gear sank to the bottom. As for the stunned Barnes and Ryan, they clung to the floating shell of the bow—speechless for the first time since they had arrived in Florida.

While the fish swam triumphantly away, nearby boaters quickly rescued the defeated anglers—anglers who never again scoffed at the fury of a tarpon.

Harrison Outerbridge

Bermuda, 1935

It was one of the greatest struggles ever between man and fish. Also one of the most shameful.

Harrison Outerbridge was fishing with some friends in the blue waters off Bermuda on a sunny, calm day in 1935 when he got a powerful strike—one so powerful that the fish jerked Harrison, who was still holding tightly to the rod and reel, overboard.

He hit the water with a big splash and quickly came up paddling with one hand while holding on to the rod with the other. "What a fish!" Harrison shouted to his stunned friends back on the boat. "This could be some kind of record!"

Furiously, he used his free hand to inch his way back to the boat while holding on to the rod with all his might. Finally, coughing up seawater, Harrison flopped over the stern and onto the deck. Despite his dunking he still felt the throb of the fish at the end of his rod.

But before Harrison could get back on his feet, the still-unseen fish gave another mighty lunge and pulled the rod out of his hands.

Harrison's eyes widened. This had to be the granddaddy of all fish. A sail perhaps? A marlin? Whatever it was, Harrison wasn't about to lose it.

Though soaked and shaken, Harrison threw himself back overboard in a determined effort to retrieve his rod. "What are you doing?" his friends shouted. "Are you crazy?"

"I'm not going to lose this fish without a fight," Harrison shouted between gulps of saltwater. "I'm going to land him if it's the last thing I ever do."

He spotted the rod zigzagging on the surface and, with a Herculean effort, snatched it. Treading water, Harrison tried to reel in the monster. But that was useless. So slowly, he struggled back to the boat without letting go of the rod. After thirty grueling minutes Harrison crawled over the stern. This time he held tightly on to the rod, got into a chair, and began reeling hard and steady.

Harrison was exhausted but confident. Nothing could

stop him now. The only question in his mind was not if he could land it but rather what he would land. With everything he'd gone through Harrison just knew he had a trophy. Still, it was strange that the fish hadn't surfaced yet.

Finally, Harrison let out a triumphant shout of joy. The moment of truth had arrived. The monster that had given the angler so much grief was about to be landed.

With one final yank of his rod Harrison pulled in his trophy. Onto the deck flopped his huge fighting fish . . . a little five-pound bonito!

Harrison collapsed out of exhaustion . . . and shame.

Jorge Martínez

Sea of Cortez, Mexico, 1978

Given a choice between catching a fish and tossing his son overboard, Captain Jorge Martínez didn't hesitate for a second —he threw his boy into the drink!

During a 1978 trip to Mexico, Al McClane, fishing editor for *Field and Stream,* wanted to go after Pacific sailfish. So he hired Captain Martínez to take him out into the Sea of Cortez. Martínez's charter boat, *El Diablo,* was the archetypal single-engine wooden boat, which the captain steered from a forward station. The boat was so rickety, McClane accidentally stuck his thumb through the transom.

Nevertheless, it was a beautiful day and McClane enjoyed the company of Martínez and the captain's nine-year-old son, Juan, who acted as the first mate. An industrious, obedient boy, Juan helped out by rigging the baits and serving lunch.

Unfortunately, by late in the afternoon there was not so much as a little tug on any of the lines. McClane was ready to give up when, to his joy, he finally got a strike. It was a feisty sailfish. Amazingly, while McClane was playing the fish, a second sailfish came up and took the bait from another line.

Captain Martínez tried to maneuver his boat without losing the two battling fish. But it was an impossible task. He had to do something—fast. After all, McClane was a world-renowned fisherman. Not wanting to lose the second sailfish, the captain grabbed his son, stuffed him into a canvas-covered cork vest, gave him one of the rods, and threw him overboard to keep the fish on the line.

"Your son! Your son!" cried a shocked McClane. "What about the sharks?"

"Oh, don't worry, señor," replied Captain Martínez. "These are the only fish we've had today, and I have more sons."

McClane, fearing for the safety of little Juan, clamped down on the drag and played the fish as fast as he could. Once McClane landed the first sailfish, the boat chugged toward the boy, who was found two and a half miles away bobbing along with the second sailfish. McClane then finished catching that fish—after first hauling in the waterlogged boy.

Roger "The Terrible" Touhy

Lake Minocqua, Wisconsin, 1930

When gangster Roger "The Terrible" Touhy went fishing, he brought along a tackle box that held more than lures and hooks. It held an arsenal of guns and bullets.

In fact, if his rod and reel didn't pull in enough fish, Touhy pulled out his fail-safe fishing gear—a Thompson sub-machine gun. Then he'd blast away at every moving fin he saw.

Touhy was a powerful bootlegger in the Chicago area during Prohibition. He made a surprisingly fine beer, which was kept in leakproof kegs built at his own cooperage. To escape the trials—both in the literal and figurative sense—of running a bootlegging operation, Touhy went on fishing trips to tranquil Lake Minocqua in northeastern Wisconsin.

However, it was seldom tranquil after he arrived. He carried enough weapons on board his rented boat to start—or end—a war. In addition to a tommy-gun and sawed-off shotgun, Touhy always packed a pistol at his side, as did many of his colleagues. Ostensibly, the guns—usually .32's—were used to put a bullet in the head of a fighting muskie after it was caught and pulled alongside the boat.

But the practice got out of hand. Touhy was one of many touchy gangsters who didn't think twice about shooting at other boats that dared encroach on his favorite fishing spots. Sometimes he got a little too trigger happy and accidentally put bullet holes in the bottom of his boat in his excitement over catching a big muskie.

The times when he didn't catch anything with a rod and reel really ignited his fury. Whenever the fish weren't biting, Touhy would whip out his trusty tommy-gun, stand up at the bow of the boat, and unload it in the water. After the smoke cleared, and the explosive echos subsided, bullet-riddled fish sometimes would float to the surface.

Even going to and from the lake Touhy liked to sharpen his shooting skills. One day Jim Ford, who as a teenager acted as a chauffeur for visiting gangsters in the Minocqua area, was driving Touhy and his thugs to the lake when the gangster ordered him to stop and pick up two hitchhiking girls. "The girls didn't know it," Ford recalled. "But they were in for the ride of their lives.

"We were driving with the windows down. Suddenly, the gangsters popped their weapons through the windows and started blasting away at those glass resistors on the telephone poles. It was practice time. I never saw two more frightened girls."

No more frightened than the fish in Lake Minocqua.

Ernest Hemingway

Off Key West, Florida, 1950

Ernest Hemingway was fishing off the Florida coast when he was shot in the leg—by a shark!

The famous author loved to fish, but he absolutely detested sharks—and his hatred for the ocean beast ballooned like a blowfish during a fishing excursion off Key West one day in 1950.

Relaxing on his boat, Ernest leaned back in his chair and dangled a line in the calm Atlantic. It had been a lazy day with nary a nibble. Suddenly . . . SPROING! . . . His line drew taut. The writer bolted up in his chair, grabbed his rod tightly, and reeled furiously, hoping he had hooked a record-size sailfish.

The battle between man and fish raged on and on. But even though Hemingway's arms, hands, and shoulders burned with pain, he refused to give up. Finally he sensed that the fish was losing its fight. Ernest smiled. But when the fish came into view, Hemingway's face turned into a mask of fury. What he'd thought was a sailfish was really a mako shark.

Ernest cursed long and loud. Then he grabbed the .22-caliber automatic pistol that he always kept aboard the boat. Determined to destroy the hated scavenger on his line, he stuck the gun in his belt and slowly reeled the shark closer.

When he pulled the mako alongside the boat, Hemingway hooked the monster with a gaff, whipped out the pistol, and aimed it at the shark's tiny brain. But the shark's wild thrashing slapped the gaff against his gun hand and the pistol went off. The bullet ricocheted off the deck—and slammed into the calf of Hemingway's leg.

Ernest quickly forgot about the mako. He turned his boat around and sped back to Key West, where he faced the embarrassment of telling his doctor that he had been shot by a shark.

Because the slug was lodged about four inches deep in Hemingway's calf, the physician decided the safest course was to leave the bullet in rather than dig it out. This gave Ernest reason to hate sharks all the more. He had detested them ever since they started snatching prize game fish from his line.

Hemingway later got his revenge by making sharks the villains in his 1953 Pulitzer prize–winning novel *The Old Man and the Sea.* But he carried the bullet in his calf until his dying day. So the shark also got his revenge—in Ernest.

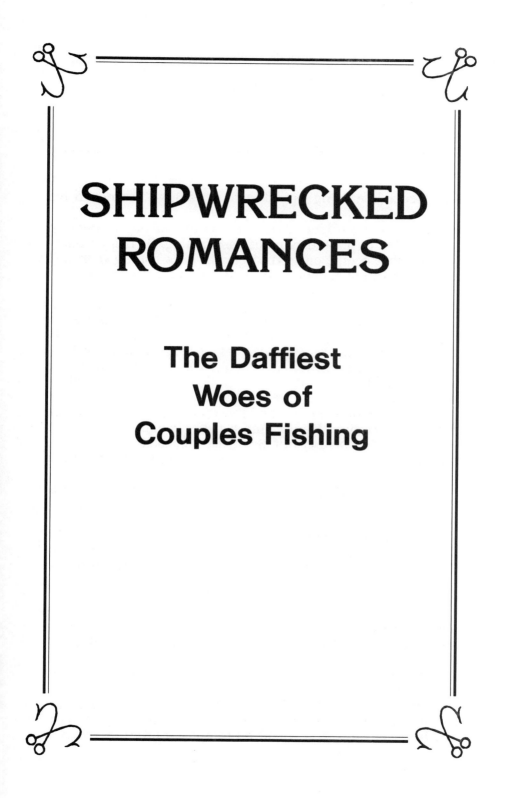

SHIPWRECKED ROMANCES

The Daffiest
Woes of
Couples Fishing

Ray Scott

Lake Eufaula, Alabama, 1970

Ray Scott is a living legend in bass fishing—but not in his own home.

Scott—the founder of B.A.S.S.—is universally recognized as the father of pro tournament bass fishing. He has probably turned more people on to the sport of bass fishing than any man alive. But as a fisherman he failed to inspire at least one person—his wife, Eunice.

Scott still remembers the day back in 1970 when the fishing was absolutely perfect. He was by himself on a three-day trip to Lake Eufaula in Alabama and couldn't have been happier. The weather was great, the lake level just right, and the bass were hitting like crazy. "I had never caught so many big bass in my life," he said. "I had ten fish that weighed eighty-six pounds."

It was all so good, he thought, that this would finally be the time to convert Eunice into a fisherwoman. She'd never been interested before, but Scott decided to drive home the ninety miles that night, pick up his wife, and bring her back the next morning.

"I figured if she started catching some of these big bass, she would get hooked on fishing and go with me on trips," Scott said.

After he showed up unexpectedly, he told her all about the fantastic fishing. But she wasn't convinced. Only reluctantly did she consent to come. "I almost had to force her into the car, but I knew once I got her there and she started catching fish, everything would be all right," Scott recalled.

"I should have suspected something when she brought along her knitting and a couple of magazines. I asked her why and she said, 'Well, if the fish don't bite I'll have something to do.'

"I remember grinning at her and saying, 'You won't need any of those things.' "

They arrived at the lake at dawn. Everything seemed perfect again. The wind, the weather, everything was just as it had been the day before. Scott hit that lake hard from dawn to black dark. He fished the same way, in the same places, as he had done twenty-four hours earlier.

And he never got a strike. Not even a nibble.

Eunice read her magazines and did her knitting, while Ray flailed away at that lake, fishing his heart out.

"I still can't explain it to this day," he said. "But it was an awfully long and quiet ride home that night. I was really embarrassed. And I don't believe Eunice ever went fishing with me again."

Ken Cook
Lake Texoma, Texas, 1982

Bass pro Ken Cook literally fell head over heels for his wife, Tammy—when he tried to show her what an expert he was at trailering a boat.

In the summer of 1982 Ken was beginning his career as a tournament bass pro and had started dating Tammy. Already he was thinking she just might be the one. But he knew that any wife of his would have to get involved with his fishing, so he took her to a tournament on Lake Texoma in Texas. On the first practice day, he decided to start her education off with a lesson on backing a boat down a ramp.

"Tammy had never backed a boat trailer down a ramp before," recalled Ken. "At the time I was driving a van, which had very limited rear visibility and made backing a boat down doubly tough. While many people use the side mirrors, I open the driver's door and lean out and watch the trailer.

"Being this great semipro fisherman at the time, and looking to impress Tammy, I told her I would show her how to back a boat down a ramp. I had her stand away so she could watch my professional technique."

Ken positioned the van just right and opened the door so he could demonstrate how to lean out and watch the trailer while backing down. Next, he carefully explained to Tammy exactly what he was about to do.

Then Ken leaned out of the van and put his left arm on the door's armrest while he looked back at the trailer. His elbow missed the armrest, however, and he fell right out of the van in a heap, almost at Tammy's feet. "There I was," Ken recalled sheepishly, "lying on the ramp, while the van and boat continued down into the water without me.

"I leapt up and scrambled to the van just in time to keep it from going all the way into the water—but I felt like a blundering fool. Fortunately, Tammy married me anyway. I guess she likes the bumbling person that I am."

Captain Joe Halperin

Great Peconic Bay, Long Island, 1974

Charter boat captain Joe Halperin spared the rod and nearly spoiled the romance.

In 1974 Joe was hooked on Diane Childress, a pretty, fun-loving, bright student at Columbia University in New York. But Diane appeared to have one big flaw, Joe thought. She was a city gal who obviously didn't know how to fish.

"We'd been dating about six months and I knew she was the one for me," Joe recalled. "But I knew I couldn't have a long-term relationship with anyone who didn't like to fish. I decided to see how she'd work out. I ordered this really neat, expensive, custom-made rod all the way from Florida. I was so proud when I presented it to her and told her how I was going to teach her how to fish."

Diane was a bit offended by Joe's condescending manner. He hadn't even asked if she knew how to fish. He just assumed that her closest encounter with a fish had been at the dinner table. What Joe didn't know was that Diane had been fishing since she was a little girl. She was an expert.

One Sunday, Joe took his sweetie out on Long Island's Great Peconic Bay in his forty-six-foot fishing boat, the *Sea Scape.* Blissfully unaware of Diane's fishy past, Joe anchored his boat near a sandbar and patiently resigned himself to a long afternoon of teaching Diane the basics of his first love. Then he set about explaining to her how to hook the bait of live shrimp. Next, he showed her how to pump the rod to hook the fish once she got a bite.

Diane gave him a dark look, feathered her line out, and let the bait hit bottom. Joe did the same thing and continued to rattle off fishing tips to her.

A few minutes later Diane expertly set the hook on a four-pound flounder and reeled it in. Proud of his student, Joe made a big fuss. "Good job! Good catch!" he shouted as he patted her on the back. "You're doing great!"

Joe rebaited Diane's line and they both cast out again. Within minutes Diane had pulled in another flounder. Then she snared another . . . and another . . . and another. By

the time Joe had caught his first fish, Diane already had six in the cooler.

Within two hours Diane was baiting her own hook and unhooking her own fish. By now she had caught a whopping total of twenty-four—while poor Joe had a mere three. It was a sunny day, but a black cloud of gloom and exasperation had descended on the skipper. He was the sailor who had fallen from grace with the sea.

When Diane reeled in fish No. 25, she turned to Joe and said sweetly, "Honey, my fingers are tired from taking the hooks out of these fish. You do this one for me."

Joe exploded. Snatching the rod from the hands of the startled Diane, Joe hurled it as far out into the water as he could.

Recalled Joe sheepishly, "All I could think of at the time was 'No damn woman is going to outfish me in my own damn boat!' And I told her so. I was enraged."

Added Diane, "It was a tantrum. I kept telling him, 'Go get my rod! Go get my rod!' But he wouldn't do it. So I stormed into the cabin and locked the door."

Although Joe felt bad, he just couldn't bring himself to retrieve Diane's rod. Fortunately, the couple eventually saw the humor in the afternoon's events and made up. But it was two months before they went fishing again. "We sort of compromised," said Diane. "We went trolling for blue marlin. We figured that if we did get a fish, we could share in the glory."

Two years later they both made the biggest catch of their lives. They got married.

Santiago Maspons

Salinas, Ecuador, 1978

"Chivalry doesn't pay," grumbled charter fleet owner Knud Holst. At least it doesn't pay in fishing. Not after a husband's good deed cost Holst's boat a world record.

Holst, whose fleet worked out of Salinas, Ecuador, was fishing with a married couple, Santiago and María Maspons, aboard his boat, the *Osprey*.

Santiago, who once held the six-pound test class record for Pacific sailfish, was using six-pound test line. Around noon one of the trolled lines started playing out slowly. Thinking it was nothing more than a small dolphin, Santiago handed the rod to his wife, María, for her pleasure.

Much to Santiago's shock a beautiful striped marlin exploded from the water seconds after he had handed María the rod. It was now María's fight to win or lose. For two exciting hours she battled the marlin until she finally and triumphantly brought it to the gaff.

Both she and her husband were thrilled beyond belief when the marlin weighed in at a whopping 144 pounds. It would have been a six-pound class world record.

But not for María. Or for Santiago. That's because if more than one person handles a rod, the fish is disqualified for the record book, according to international game-fishing rules.

When he heard the news, a disgruntled Santiago said, "I'll never hand my wife anything again."

Bob and Sylvia Warner

Nags Head, North Carolina, 1950

Newlyweds Bob and Sylvia Warner discovered that fishing and honeymoons don't mix. While she was angling for romance, he was fishing for striped bass.

They both came away empty-handed.

The two had fallen in love while working for the federal government in Washington, D.C. Minutes after Bob popped the question, Sylvia learned just what an avid angler he was. "On our honeymoon let's go to northern Ontario," said Bob, who had been fishing since the age of four. "We could camp out . . . and maybe wet a line or two."

"No," said Sylvia, whose only experience with fish was in the kitchen. "I want to go to Nags Head in North Carolina and see the dune where the Wright Brothers first flew. Besides, I want my first tumble in the hay to be on an innerspring mattress—not with a lot of wolves and polar bears trying to pull the tent down."

Bob reluctantly agreed. However, on their way to the inn on Nags Head he spotted a tackle shop and couldn't resist stopping in. He told Sylvia he'd be right back and hustled over to the shop. He returned with a surf-casting rod and all the accessories. This honeymoon was going to turn out okay after all, he thought.

After checking into an inn Bob asked Sylvia to go to the beach with him. She longed for a romantic barefoot walk in the sand. But when they reached the beach, Bob was out in the surf in a flash, casting for striped bass.

Meanwhile, a sulking Sylvia sat on a blanket, waiting for her sweetheart. Dashed were her hopes of doing their own version of the sexy beach scene in *From Here to Eternity.* Bob's mind still was solely on fishing. He waded past the first breaker, where the water was up to his knees. Then he moved farther out into the surf, until the water was up to his waist. But when he didn't get any nibbles, he walked into even deeper water until the breakers were crashing over his head.

Meanwhile, Sylvia was determined to lure him back. After looking up and down the beach and not seeing a soul, she stripped off her bathing suit. Standing completely nude, she wriggled her body seductively, hoping to tantalize him as live bait does a fish.

But Bob didn't even notice his honey mooning him. He was more interested in fishing than romancing. Rejected and dejected, Sylvia finally gave up after an hour and put her suit back on.

Minutes later Bob returned fishless. He took one look at his bride and said, "My God! You look like a broiled lobster! Thank goodness that suit covers most of you."

The sunburned bride began to cry. "I just put it back on," she sobbed. "I'm hot all over and it's all because of you. I wish I'd never married you!"

By the time they got back to the inn, Sylvia was in such pain that she went to a doctor, who gave her ointment and pain pills. That night she was in agony. Bob couldn't even touch her. The next day Sylvia began to peel, and her pain grew worse with each passing hour.

For the rest of the week Sylvia was covered with ointment and cheesecloth and looked about as sexy as an Egyptian mummy.

Today the couple, who have been married forty years, laugh about their disastrous honeymoon. Although Sylvia had every right to despise fishing, she chose to learn the sport. "It was the only way I could spend time with Bob," she said. "I'm glad I learned. Now I'm an avid fly fisherwoman."

Sugar Is Sweet, But . . .

At least one pro angler didn't find Sugar sweet.

Sugar Ferris, president of Bass'n Gals, entered a bass-fishing tournament in Arkansas in 1976. In those days women bass anglers were almost unheard of, and the tournament had neglected to provide a "men-only" provision. Of the 237 contestants who entered, Sugar was the only woman.

"When they called out the pairings, this old fisherman from Missouri heard he was paired with someone named 'Sugar,'" Ferris recalled. "He hadn't figured out yet that I was a woman. 'Where's Sugar Ferris?' he called out. I came up and tapped him on the shoulder. He looked at me as if he had seen a ghost. I swear to God, the man walked away, bent at the waist, and threw up."

Chuck Canik

Grand Lake, Oklahoma, 1983

Chuck Canik had gone to the 1983 Bass'n Gal Classic to show support for his wife, pro angler Doris Canik. But he unwittingly embarrassed her instead.

After a day of excellent fishing Doris had moved to second on the leader board, much to her husband's delight. However, Doris's engine had run a little rough, so she had the support crew pull her boat out of the water and change the plugs. When the task was done, the boat had to be launched and brought to its slip for the night.

Since Doris needed to attend a press conference, Chuck offered to handle the boat's launching. "Grand Lake was real high that year," Doris recalled. "It was so high that the water covered much of the ramp, making launching especially easy." But not as easy as she assumed.

Chuck hopped into the family Cadillac and backed the trailered boat down the ramp. Unfortunately, in his excitement over his wife's great performance that day, Chuck forgot to unhook the boat from the trailer. He kept backing down, waiting for the boat to float off the trailer. By the time Chuck realized he had backed down too far, he had gone in too deep.

"He stopped when the water started coming in over the backseat," said Doris. "But by then it was too late. He was so far into the water that he couldn't get any traction to get out. Somebody had to get a truck to pull him out."

That somebody was famed angler and TV fishing-show host Jimmy Houston. The car and boat were pulled out and the boat was relaunched—but only after it had been unhooked from the trailer.

"That was a little embarrassing, but not nearly as bad as what happened the next morning," recalled Doris. As she walked toward the slip to get her boat, she couldn't help but notice a big new sign right next to the ramp. It read CANIK'S CAR WASH and gave step-by-step instructions on how to back your car right down into the water and get it nice and clean. An employee of the Hummingbird Company (a depth finder and

169

electronics manufacturer) had erected it during the night for everybody to see.

"But even that wasn't the worst thing that happened," said Doris. "Jimmy Houston had filmed Chuck's attempt to launch the boat and the rescue of the rig. He used it to open his weekly TV show for almost a year. And, of course, I had to watch it because I like his show. So every week there was our Cadillac, with my husband in the driver's seat, being pulled out of Grand Lake by Jimmy Houston.

"I couldn't have forgotten that whole experience even if I had wanted to."

Despite the embarrassment Doris wound up winning the tournament for her first Classic victory. However, what she remembers most about the event was not her moment of fame, but her husband's moment of shame.

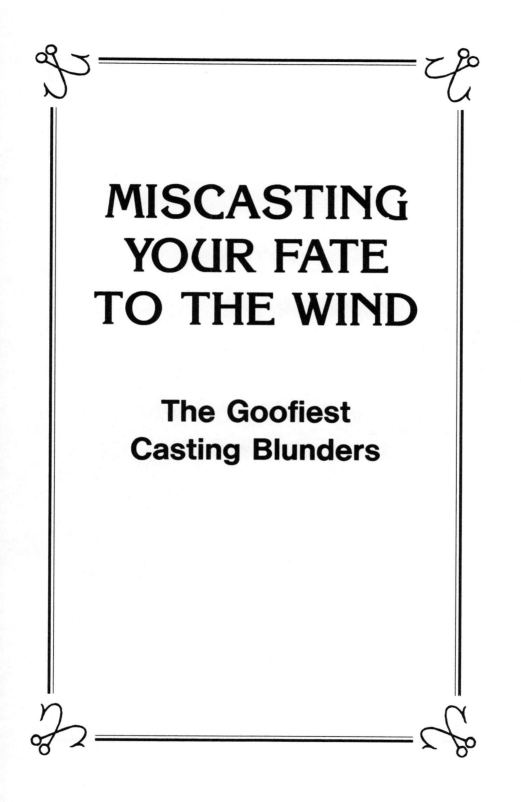

MISCASTING YOUR FATE TO THE WIND

The Goofiest Casting Blunders

Larry Nixon

Toledo Bend Reservoir, Texas, 1976

It was a cast that Larry Nixon had made a thousand times before. But in one brief moment of bad luck he hooked more than he'd bargained for—and now has a place in The Fishing Hall of SHAME™.

Nixon, the all-time leading money winner on the B.A.S.S. pro fishing circuit with about seven hundred thousand dollars through 1990, is one of the finest pro bass fishermen of all time. But even the greatest can misfire a cast in the most painful way. Nixon's ignoble incident happened when he was a guide on the famed Toledo Bend Reservoir on the Texas-Louisiana border.

"I had two customers in the boat with me when this big school of bass came up and started busting the surface right behind the boat," Nixon recalled. "I immediately grabbed a rod that I had rigged up with a top water plug and whipped a cast at the fish. And I do mean 'whipped'—that was a very limber rod. But when I whipped it back to cast, I planted the plug in the back of my head."

The hooks on the lure pierced Nixon's hat and dug deep into the back of his skull. In fact, he was stuck so badly that the barbs on the hooks were buried in his scalp.

"It had pinned my hat to the top of my head and I was bleeding like a stuck hog," Nixon recalled. "I couldn't get my hat off. And I couldn't quite reach the plug to free it. It was really a pretty bad deal."

Feeling foolish and in plenty of pain, Nixon ordered his customers to cut his hat away from his head and help him get untangled from the line. The concerned fishermen did what they were told. While still in shock over the mishap, they got another startling jolt a few minutes later.

"I was so mad at myself," said Nixon, "that I just reached back there, got a good hold of the plug, and yanked—and just ripped the lure right out. Of course, a good piece of flesh came with it. Boy, did that hurt. And it bled like you wouldn't believe. Much to my embarrassment, I had to go in and get it patched up at the hospital. And the worst part about it, darn it, was that we missed out on the fish."

John Waldman
Long Island, New York, 1980

When it's time to cast, outdoor writer John Waldman yells "Fore!" . . . while other anglers in his target range yell something else after he's sailed out one of his patented "miscasts."

Nothing is safe when he rears back with a fishing rod. But at least Waldman, a contributor to *The New York Times*, is quite candid about something a lot of fishermen would never admit—he's not a very good caster.

He had a tip-off about his affliction in early childhood—when he hooked the back of his own head on a cast and wound up in the emergency room.

But did that stop Waldman? Nope. He continued on in a fishing career that was punctuated by the bad backcast, the errant overhead, the misfire, and, well, mayhem.

"Too often my lure would pick out a wheeling gull from among the dense flocks of birds hovering over bluefish schools and hook the bird instead of a fish," he admitted. And one memorable backcast saw him hook a 180-pound St. Bernard.

But his most embarrassing cast came on a crowded Long Island Sound jetty one summer. Small bluefish were going crazy and the fishing was feverish as Waldman struck his best casting pose, aimed, and let fly—but no lure went sailing out. "I looked back in horror and saw my small silver spoon—lodged in the naked back of an old man I often saw fishing there," Waldman recalled. "To my amazement he slapped his back as if a horsefly had bitten him and continued fishing."

The chagrined Waldman then approached the old man and explained that that was no horsefly, that was his spoon. Then Waldman apologized profusely.

"The old man was not pleased to give up his fishing for

medical assistance," said Waldman. "And when I saw him later, I thought it wise not to ask for my lure back."

Charlie Biladeau
Lake Talquin, Florida, 1970

Charlie Biladeau made quite a shameful impression when he tangled with a snagged line—and lost.

Charlie was a good friend of Bob McNally when both attended the University of Wisconsin. Bob was a budding outdoor writer who wanted to follow in the footsteps of his father, Tom McNally, a well-known outdoor writer.

In 1970, when spring break approached, Bob arranged a trip to north Florida to write a story on bass fishing. The Florida Department of Tourism was only too happy to help out Tom McNally's son.

So Bob came down with his buddy, Charlie. "Like most northerners we figured we knew everything there was to know about bass fishing," recalled Bob.

Arriving at Lake Talquin, near Tallahassee, the two young men were met by a state game and fish officer who acted as their guide for the story. With the blue-ribbon treatment Bob was eager to make a good impression as a professional outdoor writer. And Charlie wanted to make a good impression as an astute fisherman.

The pair began casting plastic worms with quarter-ounce bullet-shaped sinkers at the many stumps and downed timber that dot Lake Talquin. Unfortunately, the anglers repeatedly got hung up on the logs. Even though the two were using twenty-pound test line and stiff-action rods, they kept breaking their line off on the snags.

But one snag will always be remembered and talked about. It happened when Charlie found himself terribly hung up. "He kept pulling back and pulling back, but the worm wouldn't give and the line wouldn't break," Bob recalled. "He was sitting in the backseat of the bass boat and finally he leaned way back. The line suddenly broke.

"POW! It was like a twenty-two going off. That bullet sinker came flying back and hit Charlie right between the eyes. It knocked him out of the seat and smack on his butt.

"The ranger and I were astonished."

But they obviously weren't as stunned as Charlie. He lay on his back on the boat deck, only semiconscious—with a perfectly round outline of the bullet weight right between his eyes.

"Charlie wasn't really hurt, but that outline stayed there the rest of the day," said Bob. "He didn't say a word. He just wanted to forget about the whole thing."

But Charlie Biladeau left a lasting impression. His moment of ignobility has become one of the all-time favorite true fishing stories of Florida rangers.

D. L. Holmes
and Ben Davis
Georgian Bay, Ontario, Canada, 1920

No two anglers ever got more hooked on fishing than D. L. Holmes and Ben Davis.

The two Oklahomans were in a rowboat off the Georgian Bay shoreline in Ontario, Canada, looking for bass, when they came upon a treasure trove of smallmouth. Both anglers were so excited, they lunged for their rods and nearly capsized the skiff.

The sudden lurch of the boat sent Holmes sprawling backwards over the seat. He landed with his head firmly lodged under the stern seat with his feet wildly beating the air. He was still clutching his rod in one hand. But the other hand was pinned to his knee by the hooks on his plug, which had caught on his pants.

Davis helped free his buddy and then moved to the bow, where he discovered he had been snagged by some spooners from a tackle box that had spilled open when the boat nearly tipped. By now both anglers were madly trying to get their act together before the fish disappeared.

Holmes tried to cast first, but his plug wouldn't fly because it had wrapped around the rod a dozen times and was securely fastened to the tip of the pole. He hurriedly untangled his line, attempted to whip out his first cast—and hooked Davis's rod. Davis gritted his teeth in annoyance as he freed his pal's pole.

"Now, Ben, look out," said Holmes, "for I'm gonna shoot those bass right between the eyes!"

"Look out that you don't shoot me right between the eyes," Davis retorted. "Maybe I ought to get out of the boat and stay on that island over there when you cast."

In all their excitement neither one bothered to see who would cast first. Holmes had drawn back for a mighty cast when suddenly he felt something prick his arm. Davis's plug had snagged Holmes's sweater, which was now beginning to unravel at the sleeve.

"I'm sorry," said an apologetic Davis. "Take off your sweater and I'll free my plug. The gods are against me. Go ahead. You get the first cast after all."

Once again Holmes got ready to cast. He sighted the bass, shook out his rod, aimed, and fired.

"My God, you've hooked me!" Davis screamed. Holmes wheeled around and saw that his partner was crouched in the bow with his arms wrapped around his head and blood streaming from his hand. Dangling off Holmes's plug was Davis's hat.

The plug had carved Davis's hand before glancing off and burying itself firmly into his hat. Trying to make light of the situation, Holmes said, "Very few anglers can take a man's hat off his head on the very first cast." Both broke up laughing.

Off came the plug and hat and on went another plug. "I'm going to get one of those bass if it costs me my life—or yours," Holmes declared.

Finally, he flipped his first good cast and immediately got a strike so powerful that the handle of the reel started going around too fast for him to grasp. Eventually, the whining line slowed down enough for Holmes to grab hold of the handle. He began reeling in the fish . . . but then the reel snapped off from the rod. He stared blankly at his hands. In his left hand was the rod and in his right hand was the reel.

"Drop the pole and bring him in hand over hand!" shouted Davis.

Holmes promptly dropped his pole, which quickly slid out of the boat and into the water. Meanwhile, he kept tugging at the line until the bronzeback was by the side of the boat. With a mighty yank Holmes triumphantly lifted the bass into the boat.

The angler then threw down the reel and leapt on his prey. But the reel hit the gunwales of the boat and went overboard. During all the excitement Holmes accidentally kicked open his tackle box. Plugs, hooks, spoons, swivels, snaps, sinkers, leaders, and scales landed all over the boat. Holmes tried to gather the bass in his arms, but the effort was futile. Next, he tried to sit on it, but the thrashing bass kept slithering away.

By now the struggling angler seemed to be in worse shape than the landed bass. Hooks and plugs were hanging all over Holmes. But he was so intent on subduing the bass that he didn't even notice the pricking from the barbs.

"Hit him over the head with the oar!" shouted Davis.

Holmes grabbed an oar and swung viciously at the fish. But he missed. Instead, the oar struck the gunwales and split in two. Now wielding just the handle, Holmes beat the bass to death.

Years later, the fisherman recalled the ludicrous scene: "In ten feet of water lay my rod and reel and a mess of tangled line. I picked up my sweater from the bottom of the boat. Hanging to it were behooked demons of every color and description. On my south trouser leg hung a South Bend Bass-Oreno; on the north one, a spotted Heddon. On different parts of me hung Wilson Wobblers and spoons.

"Rolling about on the stern seat was one demented, contorted, convulsed companion. And on the bottom of the boat lay one dead bass. *Veni, vidi, vici.* "

Mary Satterfield

Lake Shelbyville, Illinois, 1984

In her first bass tournament as the only woman in the field, Mary Satterfield was hoping to show the men how well she could fish. Instead, she showed them how well she could entangle herself in a hairy mess.

"I wanted to do well, but above all I didn't want to embarrass myself, since I represented the fair sex," said Satterfield, a former Lady Bass Angler of the Year. "On the morning of the tournament I was real nervous about being the only woman."

For the tournament Satterfield put up her waist-length auburn hair in a ponytail to keep it from getting in the way. Then she joined her partner in the boat and waited for the official start of the competition. Satterfield—who had five rods, each with a different lure on it—decided to make a practice cast or two while waiting for the tournament to start. She hoped it would help ease her nervousness and maybe allay any fears of her partner that she wasn't a good enough angler to be in the event.

Confidently, Satterfield flipped out a lure called a Bagley Bang-O-Lure, which had three treble hooks on it. But it got stuck on a submerged log. Trying to stay cool, Satterfield attempted to free it with a hard yank. She freed it, all right. But the lure shot back—and landed right in her beautiful long hair!

"I couldn't believe it—all three treble hooks were stuck in my hair," recalled Satterfield. "Fortunately, none of the barbs had dug into my scalp, but all nine barbs were emeshed in the hair on top of my head.

"The poor guy with me must have thought I was such a dunce. I didn't even know the man. I'd only met him the night before at the draw."

At first Satterfield inconspicuously tried to remove the hooks from her hair. But it was futile. So she swallowed her pride and asked her partner for help. But he couldn't get the hooks out either. "We struggled and struggled and all the while the fishermen in the other boats were teasing me," she said.

"I felt like every man in the tournament was watching me and thinking, *See, that's what happens when you let women in.* My partner was real nice about the whole thing, but I knew I was making a spectacle of myself. And I was taking a lot of ribbing from the other boats around us."

Satterfield, who had to let her hair down, finally freed herself from the plug just moments before the tournament got under way.

"I wondered how I'd ever redeem myself," she said. "As it turned out, I did. I caught lots of fish and came in third place. My partner didn't catch anything."

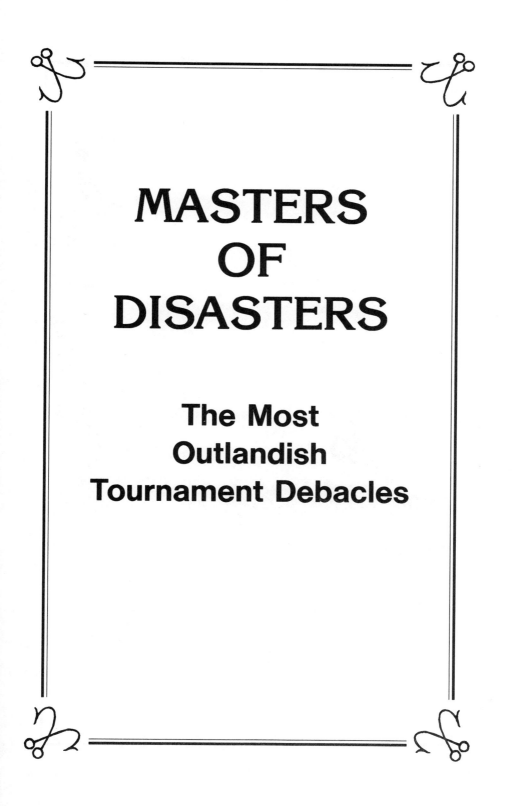

MASTERS
OF
DISASTERS

The Most
Outlandish
Tournament Debacles

Zell Rowland
1980–Present

They call Zell Rowland the "Master of Disaster" on the pro bass tournament tour—and with good reason. Accidents follow him everywhere. They're not your ordinary, run-of-the-mill mishaps. These are doozies.

"There is always something happening to me," admitted the veteran Texas pro. "I could be in the desert by myself—just me and the sand—and something bad will happen."

Take for instance the time in 1985 when he was trailering his boat through the mountains near Nevada's Lake Mead. His trailer slipped away from his car and, with the boat still snugly attached, sailed over a cliff. "I didn't notice it had popped off, but I saw everyone behind me had stopped and all of this dust was flying around," Rowland recalled. "Then I realized I didn't have a boat behind me." Although his rods and tackle survived the fall, his boat was a total loss.

At a tournament on North Carolina's Albemarle Sound in 1980, Rowland entered the final day of competition in second place. By midmorning he had caught about twenty-five pounds of bass and knew he had the tournament won. But rather than head right back for the official weigh-in, Rowland stayed out on the water all day to teach his partner some fishing techniques. Late in the afternoon, with just enough time to make the long run back to the weigh-in site, Rowland headed back—only to have the hull of his boat peel open. "The boat filled completely up to the rails in seconds and we were sitting on our tackle boxes as we idled toward shore," he recalled. "Somehow we made it, but it was dark before we got back to the ramp and, of course, I lost all of the weight I had caught that day."

Then there was the time during a tournament on Lake Mead when Rowland was paired with a local angler who knew a shortcut. Rowland tried to cut across a submerged rock island. He hit a rock ledge two inches underwater at fifty miles an hour and tore the transom out of his Ranger boat.

Rowland has suffered his share of misadventures at the boat ramp too. After a day of fishing Lake Conroe, Texas, he wiped down his trailered boat at the top of the ramp and then went inside the marina to call his wife. While he was chatting on the phone, he watched in horror as his boat and van rolled down the ramp and sank.

Recently, Rowland bought a large enclosed trailer, the kind used for racing cars. It has hydraulically activated doors so he can drive his boat right into the trailer at the ramp. That way the boat becomes fully enclosed, protected from the elements, and secure from any mishaps.

Or so he thought.

After a day of fishing at the 1989 B.A.S.S. Tournament on Sam Rayburn Reservoir in Texas, Rowland backed the special trailer down the ramp while his fishing partner, Rob Kirby, handled the boat. Kirby dutifully drove the boat into the enclosed trailer, secured it on the trailer's bow eye, and waited for Rowland to drive the truck up the ramp.

"All of a sudden I heard a loud pop," Rowland recalled. "Somehow, the retaining pin that holds the trailer hitch to the truck had come out. I looked back and there was my trailer, boat, and Rob rolling back down the ramp into the water. Then the safety chains snapped."

By now Rowland's boat and trailer were twenty feet out in the lake. He ran into the water as far as he could go, but the trailer just kept floating away. "As the trailer began to sink, all I could think about was forty thousand dollars' worth of boat and trailer going down to the bottom," said Rowland. "Then I saw Rob's head poking out the side door of the trailer. He hadn't realized he was out there floating around in the lake. Rob didn't know whether to sink, swim, or jump."

The inside of the trailer filled up with water until the boat hit the ceiling. Fortunately, the Ranger had enough flotation to keep the heavy trailer afloat. So Kirby cranked up the engine and drove the boat—and trailer—back to the ramp.

"I felt like a real fool watching my trailer get driven in like that," said Rowland. "Rob didn't have a whole lot to say. He's fished with me before and I think he knew that before the day was out, something bad would happen. To me, it always does. A black cloud seems to follow me wherever I go. I'm thinking about having a bumper sticker made up that says, ZELL'S HERE, just to warn people."

Fish Out of Water

The British Ambulance Drivers Association held its most futile annual fishing championship a few years ago.

Two hundred ambulance drivers eagerly lined up along the banks of a canal in Kidderminster, England, and began fishing in the hopes of winning the coveted title.

But after five hours not a single fish had been caught. In fact, no one had even gotten a bite.

Puzzled organizers of the tournament did some investigating —and found to their embarrassment that there were no fish in the canal!

Someone had forgotten to tell the organizers that all the fish had been removed from the canal three weeks earlier to prepare it for a new stocking.

Bill Hamilton
Arthur Smith King Mackerel Tournament, 1985

All Bill Hamilton and his buddies wanted to do was fish in the 1985 Arthur Smith King Mackerel Tournament.

But as the anglers soon found out, it would have been easier to net Moby Dick than to participate in the world-famous event. That's because everything that could go wrong did go wrong.

Hamilton, of Bennettsville, South Carolina, got up early Thursday morning with happy anticipation of enjoying the two-day tournament with three of his good friends. They loaded up his eighteen-foot boat and headed toward Myrtle Beach, thinking they had plenty of time to make the three P.M. meeting required for all the captains.

But they had hardly made it out of Bennettsville before a

wheel came off the boat trailer. Hamilton and his buddies were forced to spend the night while waiting for repairs.

It was ten A.M. Friday—two hours after the start of the tournament—before the quartet arrived at the boat ramp. Although they were a little late, Hamilton thanked his lucky stars that they had finally made it. Eagerly, he got ready to back the boat down—and wound up in his second mishap. Hamilton had untied the boat from the trailer and watched in horror as it fell off the trailer and bounced on the concrete.

But luck smiled on him—temporarily. Miraculously, the boat bounced off the ramp and into the water. A quick check showed the hull hadn't suffered any significant damage.

Hamilton breathed a sigh of relief and left his boat tied to the dock. Then he and his pals hustled over to the marina for some last-minute supplies. Now they were finally ready for some heavy-duty fishing. They walked briskly back to the dock—only to face another shock. Hamilton's boat had sunk. He had forgotten to put in the plug!

The four men worked diligently raising the boat, flushing the engine, and getting everything shipshape again. But by the time they were ready, the tournament boats were already returning. It was too late to fish the first day.

But there was always tomorrow. Hamilton had a friend who lived nearby on the Intracoastal Waterway, so they motored over to his dock to spend the night with him. It was dead low tide when Hamilton docked and tied up the boat real tight.

The quartet got up bright and early the next morning, determined to cram two days of fishing into one. After all, this was the final day of the tournament. Laden with their gear, the men marched down to the dock—only to face another shock. They found Hamilton's boat underwater again! When the tide had risen during the night, part of the boat got trapped under the dock because it wasn't tied up properly. Water from the high tide then spilled inside the boat, causing it to sink for the second time.

Hamilton and his pals spent the rest of the day raising the boat. Then the beaten men returned home, wondering if they should give up saltwater fishing for good.

Frank Baron
Ron Gabler
Jon Vanetta
Rozzie Marinelli
West Palm Beach, Florida, 1985

Members of a four-man fishing team shouted for joy when they became the first to catch all the fish they needed to claim the fifty-thousand-dollar prize in a major saltwater tournament.

But in a cruel twist of fate they came away empty-handed.

The rules for the 1985 West Palm Beach Kiwanis Fishing Tournament were simple. The first boat back to the dock with a wahoo, a bonito, a dolphin, and a kingfish would win "the richest one-day saltwater tournament in the Southeast."

The prize: fifty-thousand dollars.

More than two hundred boats set out of the Palm Beach Inlet at sunrise seeking the big money. One of them was the *Gull Seeker,* with the four-man team aboard of Frank Baron, Ron Gabler, Jon Vanetta, and Rozzie Marinelli.

At nine A.M. Baron caught a kingfish. Thirty minutes later he reeled in a wahoo. At eleven A.M. he bagged a dolphin, and forty-five minutes later he snared the bonito. The gang jumped for joy. Those fifty-thousand smackers were theirs!

"We radioed that we had them all," said Baron, who, remarkably, had caught all the fish for his team. They were the first team to radio in that they had the four fish. Now all they had to do was be the first to get back to shore.

That seemed simple enough. Gabler pointed the *Gull Seeker* for the inlet and gunned the engine. But instead of roaring off at fifty miles per hour, the boat went nowhere. It went clank . . . clank . . . clank. A frantic inspection of the engine revealed a serious transmission problem.

Of all times for the transmission to go out, it had to be now. Baron, Vanetta, Marinelli, and Gabler could hardly believe it. But all was not lost. The boat had two engines. So after a little tinkering the crippled boat limped at half power toward port, where the fifty grand awaited them.

But, alas, it was not to be. With only one engine working the *Gull Seeker* chugged a tad too slowly to the dock—and arrived just four minutes too late. To the quartet's crushing disappointment the fifty thousand dollars went to four fishermen aboard the *Shark Bait,* who, with no transmission trouble, had raced in at fifty miles an hour.

"A bummer," commented Baron. What made the losers' frustrating breakdown so ironic was that Baron, Gabler, and Vanetta worked for a company that makes parts for, of all things, transmissions!

Bassing Judgment

It was bad enough that fifty-seven anglers combined caught only one fish in the bass tournament—but then it took judges more than an hour to decide whether the fish was a winner or not.

It happened at R. D. Bailey Lake near Justice, West Virginia, in 1986.

The fishing was so bad that only one bass was brought back to the weigh-in. Depending on how it was measured, the fish was either eleven and seven-eighths inches long or twelve inches. That one-eighth inch made a big difference, because, like almost all bass tournaments, this one had a twelve-inch minimum size.

For over an hour the judges measured and remeasured the fish and closed and fanned the tail to see how it affected the size. Finally they decided it was a twelve-inch fish and awarded the first—and only—prize to the lucky fisherman.

Linda England

Lake Millwood, Arkansas, 1979

There's never a good time to hook yourself with a fishing lure—but Linda England picked a particularly bad time. So bad, it cost her a money-winning finish in a Bass'n Gal Tournament.

England, three-time Angler of the Year, was fishing in a 1979 tourney at a spot on Lake Millwood in Arkansas, where she had located a school of bass during the practice days. The school was holding tight to some hydrilla beds in open water not too far from the spot where the boats would be launched. But the fish only fed for a brief time at dawn.

"You had to be there at first light to catch them," England explained. "And I lucked out and got the second position in the first flight of boats, which allowed me to get to the spot first and on time."

She and her partner had the hydrilla to themselves. On her first cast England got a strike but failed to hook the fish. However, she snared a fish on the second cast.

As the anglers in the other boats in the tournament went by, they noticed England's good fortune. So she was in a hurry to get her line back in the water before the others tried to horn in. "I threw my first fish in the live well and ran back to the front of the boat," she said. "I was excited and in a real rush because I knew those fish wouldn't be feeding long. But if I hurried I had a chance at a limit."

First, though, England had to rip some weeds off the spoon she was using before making another cast. But in her haste she accidentally drove the hook right through her thumb.

"I couldn't believe it," she recalled. "I wasn't even worried about the pain. I just couldn't believe I had done it at a time when the fish were biting."

There stood England in excruciating pain with a big hook through her thumb while her rod handle rested on the bottom of the boat. Compounding her predicament England couldn't reach the reel to put it into free spool and give herself some

191

slack line. She was pinned right to the tip of the rod with no way to get free. She needed a six-foot arm to reach the reel.

"I yelled to my partner that I needed a little help," recalled England. "But she was so busy trying to catch fish that she didn't even turn around to see the fix I was in. She just asked what kind of help I needed. I told her I was stuck and she asked, 'Stuck to what?' That's when she turned around and almost died."

England's partner gasped and rushed over to put the reel in free spool so the hooked angler could move. Luckily, the partner was a nurse. She took one look at the hook imbedded in England's thumb and said, "We need to get you to the hospital."

England briefly weighed the importance of the tournament against her need for emergency-room treatment. She knew what she had to do.

"I'm not about to leave the tournament," she told her partner. "I'll take care of it myself." So, with the toughness of a battle-scarred soldier, England managed to push the hook all the way through her thumb. Then she cut the barb off and drew it back out until she was freed.

"But by that time the fish had stopped feeding and that really upset me," said England. Hampered by her self-inflicted injury, England finished out of the money. She rated her performance with a bloody thumb(s) down.

Rick Clunn
Lake Tohopekaliga, Florida, 1977

Rick Clunn, the only three-time winner of the B.A.S.S. Masters Classic, almost lost one of those titles over a "knotty" problem that left him red faced in front of a smirking group of outdoor writers.

It happened on Florida's Lake Tohopekaliga in 1977 when Clunn was already a successful tournament pro looking for his first prestigious Classic title. At the end of the first day of the tournament Clunn had a big lead—about eight pounds ahead of everybody else.

Since he started the next day with the lead, Clunn attracted the camera boat with its complement of outdoor writers and photographers. He also was accompanied by one of the regular press observers. (The tournament required that each contestant have a press observer on board.)

The fishing was much slower on the second day because a storm front had come through overnight. So Clunn changed from the spinner baits and buzz baits that he had used the first day to fishing a plastic worm in heavy weed cover. That is a standard postfront tactic in Florida.

About ten A.M. Clunn was flipping a weed line when he got a bite. He set the hook and immediately knew it was a big fish. Big fish means big bucks in the B.A.S.S. Masters Classic, so the attention of all the press observers was riveted on Clunn and his struggle.

"Then the line appeared to break," Clunn recalled. "Since the rod was fully bowed, the line recoiled back and shot over my head all the way to the camera boat. I looked at the press observer in my boat and told him, 'That fish broke my line.'

"But one of the writers in the camera boat was looking at my line and he shouted, 'Nope, the knot came untied.' Now, professional anglers—especially those who have a big lead in the Classic—are supposed to know how to tie proper knots." For a pro like Clunn, not tying a knot right would be like Oakland Athletics superstar slugger Jose Canseco forgetting how to hit a fastball.

"I reeled the line in from the camera boat and took a look at the end of it," Clunn recalled. "Sure enough, there was that little squiggly pigtail that proved my knot had come untied."

When fishermen screw up, most often it's when they are alone, so no one is the wiser. And even if someone should witness the foul-up, it's hardly worthy of headlines.

But not so with Clunn. Because of his stature in the sport and his bad luck of bungling in front of some of the country's top outdoor writers, his goof was news. "Those writers soon made sure the whole world knew about it when they filed their stories," Clunn recalled.

"At least I went on to win that tournament. But having that knot come untied in front of all those writers is something I don't think I'll ever live down."

Rhonda Wilcox
Lake Sam Rayburn, Texas, 1985

No pro angler in a major tournament fished so well as, yet
had so little to show for it than, Rhonda Wilcox.

Wilcox caught more big fish than she had ever snared in
her life during a tourney. It seemed as if she was the luckiest
fisherwoman at the 1985 Bass'n Gal Classic on Lake Sam
Rayburn in Texas. But, in a strange twist of fate, all her good
luck turned bad.

It started on her very first cast.

"I pitched a big old heavy worm out there and got a hit
before it even touched bottom," recalled Wilcox. "I reared back
and set the hook. My gosh! My rod bent way over double, and
the fish just started taking the drag."

Wilcox, who was using fourteen-pound test Trilene,
fought the fish to the surface, where the water began to boil
from the struggle. "All you could see was this big old silver tail
thrashing the water," Wilcox said. "My press observer in the
boat with me started yelling, 'World record! World record!'
Then the fish dove again, taking more line out."

Finally, Wilcox managed to reel the fish to the side of the
boat. But the angler was leaning back to hold the fish close, so
she still didn't know what she had caught. Her press observer
then netted the fish and slung it over the side. Wilcox's heart
pumped with the excitement of a possible world record. But
her heart sank when she examined her catch.

"It was a ten-pound-two-ounce drum—absolutely no good
in a bass tournament," she said. "So I let it go."

But what Wilcox didn't realize until later was that the fish
represented a Trilene line-class record. Had she kept the fish
and had it certified with Trilene, Wilcox would have received a
cool thousand dollars.

It was a similar story the next day.

Using twelve-pound test Trilene, Wilcox hooked a much
bigger fish than she had caught the day before. It was so heavy
that the wooden handle of her landing net broke as the press
observer hauled the fish aboard.

The fish—a striped bass—was too big to fit in the boat's

live well. So Wilcox had no choice but to lay it on the bottom of the boat, where it stayed for the next six hours while she continued to fish. Unfortunately, by having been laid out like that, the fish dehydrated and lost weight.

Again, it was a fish that didn't count in the tournament. (Only largemouth, smallmouth, and spotted bass count in such events.) But this time Wilcox had the fish certified in hopes of winning a Trilene line-class record. It weighed a whopping forty-one pounds fifteen ounces.

"But the line-class record for striped bass for Trilene was six ounces more," Wilcox said. "By the time I weighed that fish, it had probably lost almost two pounds of moisture during the hours it sat on the bottom of the boat.

"So I lost another thousand dollars."

Her bizarre luck continued to plague her.

Wilcox also caught the biggest black bass of the tournament's second day—a five-pound-twelve-ounce lunker. In most tourneys the angler who hauls in the biggest lunker wins some prize money from a lunker pot set up for each day's fishing. "But I didn't win anything for that either," said Wilcox, "because for once we didn't have a big lunker pot for the tournament."

Sadly, her three winners all turned out to be losers.

Humming a Bad Tuna

The world tuna-tossing championships have never been the same since Sharon Szabo lost an encounter with a dead tuna.

The forty-two-year-old Szabo was struck in the back by an errant toss of a fifty-two-pound frozen tuna at the 1986 world championship in South Australia.

Szabo was in a crowd watching the event when the tuna went sailing into the audience and wound up putting her in the hospital for six days. She sued the fishing town of Port Lincoln and a local fisheries group and won thirty-five thousand dollars in an out-of-court settlement in 1989.

So now organizers of the annual event use a rubber tuna to make the world safer for tuna-tossing fans.

As for Mrs. Szabo, her husband said, "We still eat plenty of tuna. Sharon says she's getting her revenge."

Cottonwood Lake Fishing Derby

Cottonwood Lake, Minnesota, 1962–Present

In 1990, at the most shameful fishing tournament in the world, it was the same old story. During the twenty-eighth annual ice-fishing derby at Cottonwood Lake in Cottonwood, Minnesota, no one caught a fish. In fact, no one has ever caught a fish in the tournament's entire history.

Not one . . . ever . . . in twenty-eight years!

"I guess there's not too many fish in our lake," admitted Larry Isaackson, secretary for the local Lions Club, which sponsors the event. "Really, nobody does too much fishing anymore."

It's no wonder. The event is now called the "Annual Fishless Derby" to reflect the futility of wetting a line in the local lake. After years of (fool)hardy fishermen braving sub-zero temperatures to sit on a frozen lake and wait for a nibble that never happened, they wised up—sort of. They still come to the derby. But now they don't even bother bringing their fishing gear.

It wasn't always that way. Originally, the tournament offered a prize for the biggest fish caught, gave away free minnows, and had holes cut in the ice with power saws for the convenience of fishermen. For several years the lake was assailed with baits of every description. But no one ever got a bite, let alone caught a fish.

In 1970 Larry Swanson, who said he had frozen a few toes (figuratively speaking) in his quest to hook a Cottonwood fish, told a local TV reporter at the event, "I'd have a better chance trying to catch a fish in the Sahara Desert. At least I'd be warm and not freezing my tail off like I am here."

Carl Andersen, of Minneapolis, a three-time derby participant, said, "If you think you can catch a fish in Cottonwood Lake in the dead of winter, then you believe in Frosty the Snow Man."

One big clue to the lake's fishing problems was discovered by the Minnesota Fish and Game Department. A study before the tournament one year found the oxygen content of the lake too low for survival of any game fish. Such news can discourage even the most enthusiastic of fishermen. But not the tournament officials. They quickly conjured up a new name for the event—"The Fishless Derby"—and turned it into a winter carnival for charity. They still have fishing, of course. It's just that no one ever expects to see an angler haul in a fish.

There was excitement in 1964 when a man brought a carp to the weigh-in. But when suspicious officials confronted him, he readily admitted he was playing a joke. The fish had been caught in another lake. After that episode there was talk that if anyone ever did show up with a fish, he should be given a lie-detector test.

But that's not likely to happen—since no one has ever caught a fish in the now-renamed Cottonwood Lake Fishless Derby.

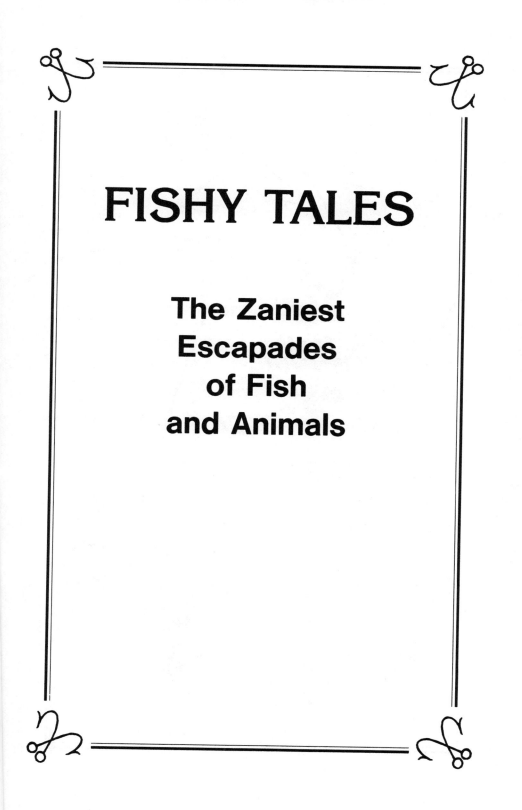

FISHY TALES

The Zaniest
Escapades
of Fish
and Animals

Marauding Marlin

Montego Bay, Jamaica, 1986

A gigantic hooked marlin showed such contempt for angler Headley Weir that it swiped four expensive rods and reels.

The larcenous marlin made its getaway on the opening day of the Twenty-sixth Annual Marlin Fishing Tournament on Montego Bay, Jamaica, in 1986.

Shortly after Weir had boarded the boat *Spritzer,* the big blue marlin struck a red-and-black softhead lure. The fish was hooked on a Penn International reel holding nine hundred yards of fifty-pound test line.

After a hard battle the marlin was brought almost close enough to gaff. It was then the fisherman realized the huge size of the fish. Captain Victor Murdock, with thirty years experience, had previously radioed that his angler had on a marlin weighing "at least eight hundred pounds." But now the fish appeared to be at least as long as the *Spritzer*'s transom— sixteen feet. That meant the marlin weighed at least an amazing twelve hundred pounds.

The marlin had no intention of getting landed. When it saw the boat, it took off on a blistering run and quickly stripped off most of the nine hundred yards on the reel. Weir fought the fish for six more hours, while the captain constantly backed the boat down on the marlin in hopes of tiring it out.

By midafternoon the seas had built up to eight feet and the battle was as fierce as ever. On its next run the big blue made it obvious that nine hundred yards wasn't going to be enough line. So, as Weir watched the last few yards of line melt from the spool, the crewmen tried a desperate measure. They snapped the swivel of an even larger rod and reel, with eighty-pound test line, onto the original reel and let it go over the side. The "rod overboard" tactic had worked for Captain Murdock in the past, but it wasn't without some risk. Each of the big-game outfits was worth six hundred dollars or more and no one wanted to lose them.

Now Weir was fighting the marlin with a second rod and reel attached to the first outfit, which was still hooked to the fish. Although attaching the second rod disqualified the fish from the tournament, everyone wanted to see the potential world-record marlin landed just to find out how big it really was.

After two more hours of struggle, the second rod and reel went overboard too, and Weir was now fighting the fish with a third outfit, another eighty-pound test setup.

By now tournament fishing was over for the day and the cocktail party was starting back at the Montego Bay Yacht Club. But no one wanted to quit aboard the *Spritzer*. Meanwhile, other crews stayed close to their radios to monitor the epic struggle taking place a few miles offshore.

As darkness fell, the marlin continued to take line, even though it was towing two rods and two reels in the water. Soon it was necessary to attach a fourth line—and the third outfit went over the side. There were now twenty five hundred yards of line out—and still Weir couldn't stop the marlin.

Despite the fact that fatigue was setting in for man and fish, neither side would give up. With the twelve-hour mark approaching, the fourth rod and reel went into the ocean and Weir was now fighting the marlin with his fifth outfit. But still, he couldn't gain line or stop the fish.

Finally, with four thousand yards of line out, the exhausted, sweaty Weir tightened the drag to try and make headway.

And that's when the line snapped.

Gone was the great blue marlin—along with two miles of line and four expensive rods and reels.

Ever since then the local islanders have believed that the mighty marauding marlin shed the hook, let the booty float to the bottom of the sea, and began looking for another fisherman to fleece.

The Best-Dressed Trout in Town

Wisconsin guide Sam Kangas caught a hefty trout in the Brule River and threw it up onto the bank, intending to pick it up later when he was done fishing.

Because it was a rather warm day for the Northwoods, Kangas took off his red sweater and threw it on the bank, too, where it landed on top of the trout.

While Kangas moved upstream, the trout thrashed about, got tangled up with the sweater, and rolled off the bank and into the river, where the fish and the sweater floated away.

For days afterward Kangas told his fellow anglers, "If you catch a trout wearing a red sweater, you can keep the fish, but the sweater belongs to me."

Bait-Snatching Birds

Orange Lake, Florida, 1980 and Lake Fork, Texas, 1987

Two ornery birds—a hungry hawk and a screech owl—literally held up fishermen in two separate crimes.

The hawk proved to be a tough old bird that not only stole a fisherman's bait but snatched his rod and reel as well. The victim was Tommy Meeks of Forest Park, Georgia, who had brought a brand-new graphite rod and bait-casting reel with him to Florida's Orange Lake in 1980.

He should have stayed home. The bass weren't biting much that day because of cold, windy weather. The forlorn angler shivered as he cast out a large shiner, hoping for a largemouth bass. Then he put the rod down in the boat and breathed on his hands to stay warm.

Suddenly, he looked up and saw a large hawk zeroing in on his shiner. The bird went into its attack mode about ten feet above the water "with claws ready to grab my shiner on the surface," Meeks recalled.

The fisherman made a quick grab for his rod, but he wasn't quick enough. The hawk grabbed the shiner and jerked the new rod and reel right out of the boat. "I was stunned," said Meeks. "At first the rod sank, but the hawk flew on and suddenly my fishing rod jumped out of the water like a big old bass."

Meeks couldn't believe what he was seeing—the hawk was flying off with the shiner and thirty feet of monofilament trailing straight down to his rod and reel. The rod skipped along the surface of the lake, sometimes rising six feet in the air as the hawk struggled to make off with its prey.

Then Meeks snapped out of his astonishment and cranked up his eighty-five-horse outboard and took off in pursuit. He wanted that outfit back.

The hawk had a two hundred-yard head start on him, but Meeks closed in on the bird, which by now had flown into a thick patch of lily pads. Each time the rod fell into the water, the big bird would find another burst of strength and power it back up over the lily pads. Meeks ran his boat wide open into the weeds and caught up to the rod.

"I was just fixing to grab it when the hawk veered off and my rod slammed against my boat," he said. The last whack did it. The line broke and the triumphant hawk continued on its way with the stolen shiner.

Meanwhile, Meeks's new outfit sank out of sight in eight feet of water. "If I'd seen it, I'd have taken a dip," said Meeks. "One thing I better not ever see again is that darn hawk."

Pro bass angler Rhonda Wilcox feels the same way about a nasty screech owl she encountered while fishing with her father on Lake Fork in Texas in 1987.

Wilcox had just caught and released a four-pound bass using a top water plug. She made another cast toward the bank and turned to her father to ask him something when, suddenly, they heard a big splash in the water. Thinking she had a strike, Wilcox turned, reared back on her fishing pole, and set the hook. To her complete surprise her line went straight up in the air.

"This screech owl—big as a fat chicken—had swooped down and picked up my bait and was flying off with it," Wilcox recalled. "Incredibly, the owl wasn't even hooked. It was clutching my plug with her claws and wouldn't let go.

"I needed that bait because it was the only one like it that I had. So I started reeling in the screech owl. I was standing in the very front of the boat with ten rods all around me and I couldn't move. So my daddy came up and grabbed the line about four feet below the owl."

The owl was not about to give up that bait without a full-fledged fight. It went on the attack. "It flew right at my face and I screamed bloody murder," said Wilcox. "I tripped over some of the rods on the deck and almost fell overboard. As the bird tried to take off, my daddy yanked on the line to bring the bird back and then he grabbed it with his hands."

While her dad held the bird, Wilcox pulled on the bait. But the screech owl still wouldn't give it up. The angler finally got a pair of pliers and had to pry the plug out of the owl's claws.

"Daddy then pitched the bird high in the air, and it flew up on a tree branch just seven or eight feet away," said Wilcox. "I could have reached up there and hit it with my rod, it was so close. The owl cocked its head and opened its eyes real wide like owls do, and it glared at us, as if to say, *You fools. How dare you try to take my food away from me!*"

"Wrong Way," the Tarpon

Folly River, Georgia, 1985

No giant tarpon so shamed its species the way "Wrong Way" did. It leapt out of the water and into a fisherman's boat—for the easiest fishing record ever.

Tarpon are legendary fighters. Their aerial displays and relentless drive make them one of the toughest fish in the water. And when an angler ties into one, he can expect a titanic battle in the water.

But "Wrong Way" sure shattered that reputation. The 142-pound tarpon was landed by stunned angler Jim Wilcox in an incredible-but-true two seconds.

However, to its credit, the tarpon did try to redeem itself with a furious rampage once it got into the boat.

In 1985 Wilcox, his buddy Bill Snow, and their guide, Fred Woodward, were fishing for speckled trout in the mouth of Georgia's Folly River. Near the end of the afternoon a medium-sized trout struck Wilcox's bait.

Meanwhile, "Wrong Way" was in the mood for a tasty morsel. As Wilcox reeled in the hooked trout, "Wrong Way" zeroed in on it too. The water then exploded and the huge tarpon soared out of the river with Wilcox's trout in its mouth.

Instinctively, Wilcox reared back on his pole. The line whipped taut and the tarpon did a flip—right into the boat. This was not where "Wrong Way" wanted to be. And it was mighty ticked off about the whole situation.

The tarpon began to thrash madly about. And unlike most bruiser tarpon that are brought to the boat, this one wasn't the least bit tired. The angry silver monster began to systematically destroy the small eighteen-foot craft.

Seats were ripped from their bolts, poles flew overboard, the boat top was shredded, and anything not securely fastened was ripped off and destroyed. For almost ten minutes Wilcox, Snow, and Woodward perched on the bow and watched anxiously as the tarpon wreaked havoc, causing about a thousand dollars' damage. "For a while there we thought he was going to sink us," Wilcox recalled.

Finally "Wrong Way" quieted down and the trio were able to return to the marina, winch the fish into a pickup truck, and get it weighed at a local seafood house with a calibrated scale.

It was a new Georgia state record, beating the old mark by almost five pounds. And it was an unofficial world record for landing a fish of that size so fast.

"Everybody's been telling me to make up a fish story," said Wilcox. "I should say I played him three or four hours and then wrestled him into the boat. But heck, don't you think the truth is pretty close to being enough?"

Rocky the Labrador Retriever

Mille Lacs, Minnesota, 1967

No ice fisherman went after a fish with more dogged determination than Rocky the Labrador retriever.

He dived through a hole in the ice, chased a pike, and then popped up through another fishing hole, much to the shock of a startled angler.

The wacky incident happened on Minnesota's Mille Lacs, where each winter as many as twenty-five hundred fishing shanties dot the lake's frozen surface. Hardy fishermen cut a hole in the ice inside each shack and fish for walleyes, crappie, and pike.

One bone-chilling day in the winter of 1967, Frank Linquist of Minneapolis brought along his pet dog, Rocky, for companionship as he waited patiently inside his shanty for a fish to take his bait. It was the first time that Linquist had let his dog accompany him on an ice-fishing trip.

The loyal Labrador lay on the ice beside the hole, curiously looking down into the icy water. Suddenly a large pike swam right across the hole, just below the water's surface. Rocky leapt to his feet, barking excitedly.

"Sshh! Sshh! You'll scare it off!" Linquist hissed.

But Rocky barked again—then jumped headfirst into the hole after the fish!

The pike darted away. But Rocky swam after it, going deeper and deeper under the thick gray sheet of ice. By the time the Labrador realized he could never catch the fast-moving fish, he was hopelessly lost and trapped.

Rocky frantically paddled here and there, back and forth, desperately searching for the hole from which he had dived. Soon his lungs were nearly bursting and his body was getting numb from the cold.

Then, up ahead, he saw a shaft of yellow light beaming down from a hole in the ice. Rocky swam toward it and veered upward. He had no way of knowing that the hole led to another shanty thirty feet away from his master's.

207

KER-SPLASH! The dog's head popped out of the water—shocking the fisherman who had been hunkered down over the hole!

The angler jumped back in surprise. In a lifetime of fishing he'd landed some strange-looking creatures, but this one beat them all.

Dog-tired Rocky finally scrambled out of the hole. Shivering from the frigid water, he furiously shook his body, showering the still-stunned fisherman from head to toe. Minutes later the diving dog and his worried master were reunited.

As for the all-wet fisherman, he went home to change his clothes. Imagine trying to explain that catch to your angling buddies: "Well, fellas, it was four feet long, had big ears, was covered with hair, and . . ."

Old Lead Belly

Sandy DeFresco couldn't believe her eyes when she hauled in the largemouth bass of a lifetime from the Miramar Reservoir outside San Diego. When weighed back at the dock, it registered twenty-one pounds ten ounces, a new California state record, and instant celebrity status for Sandy.

But her stardom didn't last long. When taxidermist Jamie Lyons opened the fish up a few days later, he found a two-pound eight-and-three-quarter-ounce lead weight inside the fish.

With the lead out, the fish weighed "only" nineteen pounds one and a quarter ounces. Although it was still a big bass, it was well under the twenty-one-pound-three-ounce state record.

Apparently, "Old Lead Belly" decided to scarf down a heavy meal and swallowed the weight, which had been lying on the bottom of the reservoir.

"Big Mo"

Lake Ray Hubbard, Texas, 1986

In a shocking display of overindulgence a striped bass known as "Big Mo" carried a mouthful of not one but two lures while dragging a rod and reel.

It was a glutton for punishment.

"Big Mo" was a striped bass that lived in Lake Ray Hubbard near Dallas, Texas, where Bill Cork was fishing with good friend and guide Rex Bridges.

In only an hour's fishing that morning Cork and Bridges caught and released twenty or thirty stripers, all in the three- to six-pound range. Then Bridges announced it was time to try for "Big Mo"—his name for each of the big stripers that swam in the middle of the lake.

On the way out the anglers pulled up alongside a bass boat belonging to *Field and Stream* fishing editor Ken Schultz. After exchanging pleasantries Schultz somewhat sheepishly told them, "If you catch a world-record striper—with a rod and reel attached—it's mine."

Seeing the bewildered look on their faces, Schultz explained, "I had been trolling just before you got here and I had a gigantic strike—one so powerful that it snapped my rod in two just below the reel seat. The rod and reel shot overboard, leaving only a piece of the handle in my hand. That must be a world-record fish to snap a sturdy Fenwick rod like that."

Schultz, still upset at losing the fish as well as a brand-new rod and reel, then headed back for the marina for lunch while Cork and Bridges rigged up for trolling. "I'm going to try to catch Ken's fish and not only break a world record, but retrieve his rod and reel too," Cork told his fishing partner. Bridges reminded him that the world-record freshwater striped bass was sixty-six pounds, and the Texas state record was over forty-three pounds.

As the anglers pulled in some eight- to ten-pounders, Bridges began needling Cork about trying to catch a world record. Cork recalled what happened next:

"Just then I had a strike and set the hook. The fish fought strangely. At times I thought maybe I was snagged—there were no rapid dives, no long runs, no violent tugs. But I knew I had something big on and it seemed to be alive. Suddenly the tip of a fishing rod emerged from the water. I stared unbelievingly as I retrieved a broken rod and reel . . . could this be Ken's rod I had snagged?

"But there was still a slight tugging on the line, so I knew there was something else on and sure enough—a striped bass came up next. Incredibly, it had two lures in its mouth—my lure and Ken's.

"I couldn't believe it. I had caught Ken Schultz's 'world record' fish . . . with the rod, reel, and lure still attached to the fish! How could that fish have struck another lure with all that junk trailing out of its mouth?"

It was a pigged-out "Big Mo." The striped bass weighed eleven and a half pounds, a decent fish but hardly one of rod-breaking proportions. In the fish world it definitely was a hog.

They put "Big Mo" in the boat's live well, with the rod and reel still attached to it, and took off for the marina to try and catch Schultz. He was just walking back to his boat when they arrived.

"Have any luck?" Schultz asked.

Cork simply held up the rod and said, "Recognize it?"

Schultz froze. Then he hustled toward their boat, but stopped again when Cork picked up the reel and asked, "Is this yours?"

Schultz's heart was pounding. "Where's the fish?" he asked excitedly.

Cork reached in the live well, held up the not-so-big "Big Mo," and goaded, "Here's your world record."

Schultz shook his head in disbelief—disbelief the fish had hit twice . . . and disbelief it was so small.

Cork gave Schultz back his reel but was allowed to keep the rod and the fish. "Big Mo" was then mounted with the two lures in its mouth. Said Cork, "It now hangs on my office wall —along with the broken rod. They're a constant reminder of just how crazy fishing can be."

The Unknown Salmon
Juneau, Alaska, 1987

A salmon that allowed itself to be caught by a hungry bald eagle unwittingly grounded a commercial jetliner.

In 1987 the salmon was swimming peacefully in a river near Juneau, Alaska, when the eagle swooped down, caught the delectable fish, and went flying off toward its aerie with the salmon firmly clutched in its talons.

Suddenly, the bald eagle spotted another giant bird heading straight for it—and the scaredy-cat eagle decided it was best to relinquish its prey and flee for its life.

Talons flew open and the salmon fell through the air. The fish then smashed into the cockpit window of the bigger "bird"—an Alaskan Airlines Boeing 737 that had just taken off from the Juneau airport.

Concerned about possible damage, the pilot of the Anchorage-bound jetliner made an emergency landing in Yakutat two hundred miles away, where mechanics made a careful inspection.

"They found a greasy spot with some scales, but no damage," said Paul Bowers, the Juneau airport manager.

The flight's forty passengers were forced to cool their heels for about an hour before the plane was pronounced airworthy and allowed to continue on to Anchorage.

The bizarre incident went down in aviation history as the first-ever midair collision between a commercial jetliner and a fish. The eagle apparently escaped injury.

As for the fish, it is missing and presumed dead. Some people believe it's buried in the Tomb of the Unknown Salmon.

The Monster Marlin
Mombasa, Kenya, 1985

Like a monster from the deep, a crazed big blue marlin soared out of the water and crashed headlong onto the deck of a ferry, sending passengers fleeing in panic.

Pandemonium broke out aboard the boat near Mombasa, Kenya, after the giant marlin smashed into a crowd of startled commuters on the ferry. The passengers—not realizing exactly what had hit them—scattered in all directions as frightened women screamed, "Monster! Monster!"

So afraid that it was a sea monster, the passengers charged to the other side of the boat and nearly capsized the ferry. "We have been invaded by a monster from the deep!" shrieked a commuter.

Finally, a few brave souls crept back toward the wild behemoth that was thrashing about, banging on the deck, and slashing at everything in sight with its wicked sword. They sighed with relief when they discovered that it was no monster but only a big blue.

The fish apparently had been disturbed by the throbbing of the ferry's diesel engines, causing it to jump out of the water. Unfortunately, its timing was bad, because it landed on the deck instead of back into the drink.

When word spread that the invader was a giant marlin, the crowd surged toward the fish. They no longer feared the marlin; they hungered for it. Some of the more courageous passengers tried to kill it for food. Determined to beat the marlin into submission, they assaulted the fish with sticks, pocketknives, and even shoes. Attackers were tossed about right and left by the furious fish, but others managed to hang on grimly until more joined the fray.

Eventually, the marlin lost the battle, more because it was a fish out of water than from being beaten. When the ferry docked, the victors took their trophy to a nearby shady area, where the monster was cut down to size and eaten.

Singing Blowfish

Richardson Bay, California, 1985

For years houseboat dwellers on San Francisco's Richardson Bay were driven daffy by a mysterious, irritating *Hummmmm* that kept them awake all night long.

Nobody knew what was causing the eerie drone—variously described by residents as similar to an electric razor only ten times louder . . . or a powerful generator . . . or a squad of low-flying B-17 bombers.

The only thing certain was that it came and went like clockwork every night of every single summer.

Each evening, as though a light switch had been thrown, the *Hummmmm* began. At midnight it peaked in loudness and at dawn the noise clicked off.

Frustrated houseboaters suspected the source was everything from a sewage plant . . . to secret government experiments . . . to visiting aliens from outer space—aliens enjoying a summer vacation on the picturesque bay across from San Francisco.

But absolutely nobody suspected the noise was really a chorus of underwater mating calls—from love-starved fish!

For years people had tried to track down the hum. It wasn't until 1985 that baffled county health officials finally hired a team of sound engineers to locate the hum's source once and for all. But at first even the experts had no luck.

One engineer, Stephen Neal, paddled around the bay in a small rowboat tracking the hum with listening devices dropped into the water. He came up with this interesting conclusion: "The sound appears to come from nowhere."

Then Thomas Niesen, a marine ecologist at San Francisco State University, heard a TV report about the hum. Remembering some earlier studies he'd done on fish noises, Niesen phoned the engineering firm and asked them to play him a tape of the bay hum.

"It was like déjà vu," said Niesen. "There was no doubt that this was the sound of the plainfin midshipman, which is also known as the singing blowfish."

Sound engineers caught some blowfish in the bay, lis-

215

tened to their "singing"—and, sure enough, discovered they were the culprits!

The male blowfish advertises for mates by vibrating a stomach bladder up to 150 times a second—and when hundreds, possibly even thousands, of blowfish are singing at once, the sound is deafening.

One fish expert said he was amazed that no one had suspected a living marine creature before. After all, he noted, "What's looking for romance at night and in the summer? Not machinery!"

But even though the mystery was solved, there was still no relief in sight for the houseboaters. Scientists couldn't come up with a solution to stop those things that go hum in the night.

HOOKS, LINES, AND STINKERS

The Nuttiest Blunders in Fishing

Richard Bowles
Madison, Wisconsin, 1954

Richard Bowles turned the simple act of cleaning fish into a neighborhood nightmare.

He dumped the fishy remains in a garbage can, where they rotted and raised a horrid stench—a goof that wrecked a backyard barbecue, infuriated garbagemen, sent firefighters on a false alarm, and nearly got two of his pals arrested.

And the chain-reaction disaster resulted just because Bowles, outdoor editor for the Gainesville, Florida, *Sun,* decided to do a good deed.

In 1954 Bowles visited Madison, Wisconsin, where he had graduated from the University of Wisconsin, and enjoyed a great day's fishing on Lake Mendota. He caught four nice walleyes and took them to the home of a favorite professor and his wife, Dr. and Mrs. Samuel Burns. He thought the couple would enjoy the fillets.

Bowles cleaned the fish in the Burns's backyard, wrapped the carcasses in newspaper, and stuffed them into a paper bag. Then he told Mrs. Burns, "If you'll give me a shovel, I'll bury this in the back corner of your garden."

"That won't be necessary," she said. "The trashman comes tomorrow. Just put it in the garbage can." So Bowles dumped the bag in the metal can and closed the lid.

Unfortunately, both Bowles and Mrs. Burns forgot that the next day was July Fourth—and the garbage truck wasn't scheduled to return for eight days.

Bowles left town the day after cleaning the fish. He didn't return to Madison until a year later—and that's when, over dinner, the Burnses filled him in on the week of wacky events that followed his discarding of the fish remains.

"The stench was unbelievable," Mrs. Burns told him. "Our back-fence neighbors had guests coming that week for a backyard cookout. They circulated through the area looking for the source of the foul odor, thinking there might be a dead body hidden nearby.

"It was quite humiliating when they zeroed in on our garbage can! We then put the can in our garage, closed the doors tight, and left it there until the next garbage pickup."

When the Burnses finally opened the garage a week later, they found maggots all over the place. Holding their noses, they dragged the stinking can out to the curb and spent the morning cleaning up the garage.

The garbage truck came that afternoon—and when the garbagemen got a whiff of the evil-smelling can, they nearly had a heart attack from the overpowering stench.

"The truck stopped and two men walked up to the can like it was a wild animal," Mrs. Burns told Bowles. "One of them yanked off the lid and they both leapt back as if there was a fire in there. They carried the can at arm's length, suspended between the two of them. After they'd dumped the can into the truck, one of them saw me watching. He called out, 'Lady, you should be ashamed!' "

Once the can was empty, Mrs. Burns and her hubby let it air out for a few hours. But it still stank to high heaven. And the drama wasn't over yet.

They got a garden hose and thoroughly rinsed out the can. Still, the horrible odor kept swirling about them like a putrid cloud. They scrubbed the can with the strongest disinfectant soap they could find. But the can was still a menace, and angry neighbors were about to raise an even bigger stink.

A neighbor came over and suggested they put some dirt in the bottom of the can, splash in a little gasoline, and let it burn for a while, Mrs. Burns told Bowles.

With that said she rose from the table and pointed out a window. Bowles followed her finger and saw a neat brown circle in the backyard. "That's where we built the fire in the garbage can," Mrs. Bowles said.

"When we tossed a match into the can, the gasoline ignited with a great WHOOSH! and flames leapt high in the air. Somebody called the fire department and firemen arrived, making a great commotion. By that time the fire had burned down, but smoke was still coming out of the can. They squirted it with a fire extinguisher and told us that open fires were prohibited in residential areas. But after we told our story, they decided not to arrest us."

Dr. Burns finally got rid of the Garbage Can from Hell by borrowing a friend's pickup truck and personally hauling it to the city dump, his wife said. "But even when he rolled it off the truck, it still stank!"

Said Bowles: "After the Burnses told me their story, I was overwhelmed with shame. But luckily they were chuckling about the bizarre tale."

U.S. Postal Service
Tulsa, Oklahoma, 1989

When Dan Kadota mailed in his entry for a nationwide fishing contest, he had high hopes of winning. But then those hopes were torpedoed by the U.S. Postal Service.

Kadota would have won the fifty-thousand-dollar prize easily had his entry not been mangled by the Tulsa post office.

The angler's incredible tale began on January 2, 1989, when he mailed off his entry fee and application to *Bassin* magazine's Big Bass World Championship contest. First prize of nearly fifty thousand dollars would go to the fisherman who entered the contest and caught the largest bass of the year. Kadota, who runs charter boats out of Los Angeles and San Diego for a living, has a passion for big bass fishing, and he thought his chances were as good as anyone's.

Six days after mailing in his entry he went fishing . . . and hauled in the bass of a lifetime—nineteen pounds four ounces—with a live crawdad on Lake Castaic, California.

"I thought I had the contest locked up," Kadota admitted. He quickly had the fish weighed on certified scales and mailed off the paperwork to both *Bassin* magazine for the big cash prize and the International Game Fish Association for world-record status.

In no time at all Kadota heard from the IGFA, which confirmed he had broken the world record for bass using twenty-pound test line. Great, he thought. Now for the fifty thousand dollars.

Exactly two weeks after submitting his contest entry Kadota got a letter from Tulsa, Oklahoma, where the magazine is located. But it wasn't from *Bassin* magazine. It was from the U.S. Postal Service. The letter was an apology. It said that apparently the post office's sorting machine had accidentally chopped up a letter of his and couldn't be delivered, so it was being sent back. Kadota warily looked in the envelope. Inside were the remains of his check and entry form for the Big Bass World Championship.

"I couldn't believe it," Kadota said. "I was stunned. I had never had a piece of mail returned like this before in my entire life. Why this piece?"

He immediately called the magazine and found the editors sympathetic to his plight. They even sent their lawyers to the Tulsa Post Office to see if something could be done. When told of the situation, an unfeeling postal official coldly replied, "We accidentally chop up three hundred pieces of mail a day in our sorting machines here. What's the big deal?"

It was a very big deal to Kadota. The magazine disqualified his fish because the rules stated that entries had to be received before the paperwork on any potential winning fish could be submitted.

"I was upset, of course, but at least I had the world record," said Kadota. "However, I couldn't believe the attitude of the post office. I think that infuriated me the most."

Some anglers might have quit at this point—or gone hunting for a postmaster. But Kadota just sent in another entry—by registered mail this time—and went back to fishing. Over the next ten months he continued to catch big bass— fourteen of them over ten pounds. None of them, however, came close to the then current contest leader, a fifteen-pound-two-ounce bass out of Texas.

Then in December, with the contest only a few weeks from ending, a miracle happened.

"I was back on Lake Castaic, fishing live crawdads, and I had already caught one bass that day that weighed over twelve pounds," recalled Kadota. "Then I got another strike. I knew from the start it was a really big fish. In no time I had it in the boat.

"The first thing I thought when I saw that fish was *There is a God.* I knew the contest was going to be close, but I thought I had the winner."

He had landed a fifteen-pound-four-ounce bass. Again, Kadota sent in the necessary paperwork—by registered mail, of course. "I had to sweat out sixteen days to the end of the year," he said, "to see if my fish would hold up."

It did. Kadota won the 1989 contest by a mere two ounces —and pocketed the prize of $47,025. When he received the wonderful news, he asked one favor of the magazine: Please don't put the check in the mail.

Dave Davis
Wheeler Lake, Alabama, 1975

Sometimes it just doesn't pay to be a Good Samaritan—as Alabama wildlife officer Dave Davis found out when he tried to fix a fishing reel for a little old lady.

Davis was checking anglers for their fishing licenses on Wheeler Lake in Limestone County in 1975 when he noticed a little old lady with an old Zebco closed-face reel. She was having difficulty casting.

"She couldn't cast her line out more than ten or twelve feet, which really wasn't getting her where she could catch fish," Davis recalled. "So I decided to help her. She let me take her reel apart, check it out, and put it back together.

"I hadn't really found a problem, but I thought just taking it apart might have helped, so I said to her, 'Ma'am, let me try this for you, please.' She had a rig with a sinker at the end of the line and a couple of hooks farther up."

Davis reared back and let it fly. The line went out all of fifteen feet, caught on something inside the reel, came flying back . . . and wrapped around the little old lady a half dozen times!

"The line was all wrapped around her legs and ankles," Davis recalled. "I had to unwind her from the line. The lady didn't say a word, but I could tell she just wanted me to go away. Meanwhile, the banks of the lake were lined with people fishing—and they were all staring at me.

"I felt like an idiot."

That wasn't the first fiasco Davis experienced in his eighteen years in the Alabama outdoors. He splashed right into a moment of shame during his first year as a wildlife officer in 1972.

"I was paired with a veteran officer named John Clowdus, who was a real Alabama 'good ol' boy,' " Davis recalled. "We were checking fishing licenses around Guntersville Lake when we spotted two young ladies in bikinis. They were fishing at the end of a fifty-foot-long public pier and they looked great from a distance. We pulled over and John looked at me and said, 'Go get 'em, son.'

"I was a six-foot-tall, 235-pound ex–football player who felt pretty good striding down that pier in my uniform—until I got about three quarters of the way down.

"Just as I neared the girls, the pier collapsed under me and I plunged into the water, which was about eight feet deep. I treaded water, desperately trying to hang on to what little dignity I could. The two girls leaned over the remnant of the pier and asked, 'Are you okay?'

"They were too small to pull me out and I just told them I was fine and said, 'You ladies have a nice day.' I managed to climb up the shore side of the pier.

"With as much dignity as I could, I trudged back down that pier to the car with water squishing out of my boots and out of my clothes. I could see Big John just sitting in the car at the end of the pier staring at me.

"Instead of asking if I was all right, the first thing Big John said to me was 'Dad blame it, boy, that embarrassed the hell out of me.' "

Jack Rothwell
Chesterfield Canal, Nottinghamshire, England, 1978

Thanks to dredger Jack Rothwell, a good day of fishing for three anglers went down the drain.

In the summer of 1978 Rothwell was in charge of a team that was dredging the Chesterfield Canal near Retford in Nottinghamshire, England. At the same time nearby, Howard Poucher, Graham Boon, and Pete Moxon were happily fishing from the canal bank. While waiting for the fish to bite, the trio watched Rothwell's cleanup crew use grappling hooks to haul up submerged rusty bicycles, refrigerators, and other junk that littered the canal floor.

The crew then struggled with an especially heavy iron chain lying on the bottom. They couldn't budge it. Finally, Rothwell ordered the chain to be hooked to a corner of the dredger. Driver Kevin Bowskill started the huge machine and it quickly freed the iron chain. The crew hauled in the chain, which had a large block of wood on the end of it, and deposited the junk on the canal bank for pickup later. Then they knocked off for lunch.

Suddenly, the three fishermen noticed a change in the canal water. First, the current appeared to be moving a little faster than before. Then it seemed as if the current was moving very fast.

Finally, right before their eyes, a gigantic whirlpool formed in the normally placid canal—and started sucking up all the water.

One of the fishermen ran for the dredging crew, but by the time they returned, the canal had run completely dry. As the fishermen and workers stared at the now waterless canal, they finally figured out what had happened.

The dredgers had pulled the plug!

The plug had been put there two hundred years earlier by engineer James Brindley, when he built the half-mile-long waterway, and it had lain there undisturbed ever since. Now the millions of gallons of water that had filled the canal had rushed into the nearby River Idle. All that was left in the canal were a few pools of water, some grounded pleasure boats

225

stranded at their docks, the dredger now stuck firmly on the bottom, and lots of rusty junk.

And flopping fish.

At first Poucher, Boon, and Moxon were angry over losing their favorite fishing spot. But as they looked at the marooned roach and perch, they quickly made the best of a bad deal and gingerly jumped down in the mud and scooped up dinner.

And they had a wacky fishing tale to tell as well. For once, it wasn't the fish that got away, it was the water.

Brevard County Jail Inmates
Indian River, Florida, 1982

Crime not only doesn't pay, it doesn't do much for the outdoor instincts of criminals either. A well-intentioned plan to let prisoners go fishing flopped shamefully when the convicts plotted to escape instead.

It seemed like such a good idea—let jail inmates out to go fishing under supervision in the fish-rich Indian River and use the catch to keep the jail food-bill down.

But it didn't work.

"I didn't know how dumb some of these cons were," said Sheriff Jake Miller, of Brevard County, Florida, where Cape Canaveral is located. "You take for granted that fishing comes natural to most people. But for some reason it doesn't come natural to people in jail."

Sheriff Miller's plan was simple: let the inmates use the department's seventeen-foot boat to fish for mullet, which are plentiful in the saltwater estuary known as the Indian River. The sheriff thought it would be good for them to get out—and good for the department's food budget.

"It was our intent to catch enough to feed the inmates fish twice a week and save fifteen to twenty thousand dollars a year," said Miller. "The plan was to send two or three nonviolent 'model' inmates out in a boat with a thirty-five-horse motor.

"When you fish mullet in the Indian River, you fish in shallow water near shore. You don't have to go very far to catch them, so you don't need much gas.

"The first group we sent out tried to con the guards into giving them twelve gallons of gas—that's almost enough to take them to Cuba. They were planning to escape."

Sheriff Miller put a stop to those thoughts by limiting the boat to just one gallon of gas, which was plenty for fishing the Indian River. The prisoners never tried an actual escape attempt. They also never caught any fish.

"I'd find those cons sitting in the boat out in the middle of the channel in thirty-foot-deep water," recalled Miller. "You're not going to catch mullet in the middle of the channel.

"Instead of fishing, these guys were trying to beg fish from real fishermen passing by in their boats!

"Well, after about six months I canceled the program. Between the cons who were hoping to escape and the others who were too dumb or too lazy to catch mullet, it just wasn't productive. So much for that idea."

Clyde Slonaker

Sand Creek, Colorado, 1959

Colorado wildlife officer Clyde Slonaker's biggest arrest backfired on him because he was stuck "cleaning up" the case till the wee hours of the morning.

Slonaker was patrolling Sand Creek in Colorado near the Wyoming border. The creek held excellent brook trout, especially since it was the beginning of the fishing season right after the snow melt. The trout weren't large, but they were plentiful. Sand Creek was the perfect place for those hardy fishermen willing to bust through the snowbanks and mud holes to get to the remote creek.

Most fishermen there enjoyed catching the trout and releasing them once they reached their limit. But there were always the greedy ones, and Slonaker kept a lookout for them.

One day in 1959, early in his long career, the officer followed car tracks into the creek area and found two vehicles parked near an old abandoned cabin. Slonaker hid in the brush and soon saw a fisherman emerge from the creek and bury a sack in a snowbank near the cabin. Then another angler showed up and did the same thing. As the afternoon wore on, Slonaker saw six different fishermen come out of the creek and bury sacks in the snowbank.

At the end of the day, after the men had set up around a campfire, Slonaker emerged from the brush and asked to see their fish. The anglers took him to a different snowbank, where they brought out sixty trout; each fisherman had his limit of ten.

The officer then walked over to the other snowbank and asked them what they had hidden there. At first they pretended they didn't know what he was talking about. But when he told them he had watched them all afternoon, they resignedly pulled out the bags.

Slonaker wasn't prepared for the bonanza—356 illegal trout came out of that snowbank, the biggest fish seizure of his thirty-five-year career. He quickly wrote out summonses for the men and took the 356 trout home with him.

And that's when he learned his lesson.

"It was eleven P.M. by the time I got home, and then it hit me," Slonaker recalled. "I couldn't let all that fish go to waste. I had to clean every one of those 356 fish. There was no snow around my house to bury them in and I had no place to store whole fish. So my wife and I stayed up until the wee hours of the morning cleaning those trout.

"From then on I made the fishermen clean the fish before I confiscated them as evidence."

Jack Daniel's Distillery

Mulberry Creek, Tennessee, 1987

Anybody going fishing in Tennessee's Mulberry Creek on the morning of July 17, 1987, should have used a hangover cure as bait—because the day before, all the fish got sloshed to the gills!

Suckers, minnows, and other fish were diving while intoxicated after a broken pipe at the famous Jack Daniel's Distillery leaked 13,800 gallons of whiskey into the creek, located near Lynchburg.

"As much as a mile downstream you could pick out the smell as being Jack Daniel's liquor," said biologist Dick Williams of the Tennessee Wildlife Resources Agency. "And those fish downstream were swimming kind of sluggish."

Some of the smaller fish had a shamefully low tolerance for the aged Tennessee sippin' whiskey, and when the big binge was over about one hundred tiny finnies were finito.

Nobody knows if the fish that survived ended up with hangovers. But plenty of painful groans were heard coming from the distillery, because the lost liquor was worth a whopping seven hundred thousand dollars.

That wasn't the first time marine life has gone on a bender. In 1933 game wardens discovered huge numbers of fish floating on the surface of New York's Ellicott Creek—all as stiff as boards.

The wardens carried some of the fish that were still alive to another nearby creek, where they soon regained consciousness. Officers observed that the fish looked hung over as they swam away . . . very slowly.

When government prohibition agents learned about the strange incident, they knew something was fishy. They checked the creek banks and upstream discovered an illegal still. (Prohibition hadn't been repealed yet.)

Moonshiners had dumped a thousand gallons of intoxicating mash into the creek . . . and that's why all the fish were fried.

Michael Baughman

1981

All fly fisherman Michael Baughman hoped to do was make streamer flies out of skunk hair. Instead, he stumbled into an ordeal that stank to high heaven.

Baughman was innocently driving home from a fishing trip one day when he spotted a dead skunk on the side of the road. Baughman, who loved to tie his own flies, had long heard that the coarse hair from a skunk's tail is better than bucktail for tying streamer flies.

He had checked out skunk road-kills before, but they had been either too smashed or too odorous. This one looked pretty good, so he stopped, backed up to it, and rolled the window down. The dead skunk appeared in good shape and a quick sniff failed to detect an odor.

At last Baughman found the skunk tail he'd wanted. He parked and, with pocketknife in hand, gingerly approached the skunk. As Baughman grabbed the tail, he noticed there was an odor after all, but it wasn't too bad. He started hacking away at the tail, but the dull knife made progress slow.

As he slashed at the tail, the smell grew steadily worse. By the time the angler was halfway through, it was so bad, he had to hold his breath. When he couldn't hold it any longer, Baughman sprinted twenty yards down the road and took a big gulp of fresh air. Then he went back to the tail.

After five minutes of sprinting, gulping, sprinting, holding his breath, cutting, then sprinting again, Baughman's patience wore thin. He decided a quick hard yank would probably sever the tail.

The tail didn't come off, but a jet stream of greenish-yellow liquid did. It shot out from the dead skunk and completely drenched Baughman.

"It was the most powerful natural force I've ever encountered," said Baughman, writing in *Sports Illustrated*. The angler staggered away, blinded by the spray and overwhelmed by the smell. He ended up behind his car, bent over, gasping for breath and shaking his head to clear his eyes. After half a minute he could see again, but barely. Discarding his wet

231

jacket, which had taken the brunt of the spray, he abandoned any further thoughts about the skunk and stumbled to the car.

Baughman was in a stinking mess. He had a hundred miles to go, he was saturated with skunk juice, and the smell was getting worse. He rolled down all the windows and even stuck his head out as he drove, but the smell went from staggering to retchingly repulsive.

He knew he had to do something or he'd never make it home. Then he remembered a skunk-smell antidote used on dogs—tomato juice. Why not? If it helped man's best friend, it should help man, he thought.

So Baughman pulled up to the gas pump of the first country store he saw and stepped out of the car. An elderly attendant approached but then stopped at twenty feet and sniffed.

"Skunk," called out Baughman.

"Just one?" asked the old man.

Baughman knew better than to move any closer to the attendant. He asked the old man to bring out six large cans of tomato juice. The attendant agreed but asked Baughman to move farther away from the store. The man placed the cans by the side of the road and then stepped back as Baughman took the cans and left the money behind.

With the mission accomplished Baughman continued on, looking for a place to take a tomato-juice bath. Fortunately, he found a deserted forest service campground and promptly wheeled in and strode to the rest room. Inside he quickly stripped naked and began to slowly empty all six cans—twelve quarts—of juice over his head. The sticky liquid oozed down his body, and he rubbed it around as best he could, then waited for the effect. But there was none.

Baughman now smelled like a skunk who had taken a bath in tomato juice.

He turned to the sink to wash the sticky liquid off. But, alas, there was no water. Seized with a feeling of impending doom, Baughman tried all the sinks, but since it was still early spring, the water hadn't been turned on yet. So he put his clothes back on and slunk out to the car, praying he wouldn't meet anybody. By now he was enveloped by a repulsive odor and had a reddish cast to his skin and hair.

Baughman headed back down the road and reached the interstate as night fell. Because it was cold, he had to roll his windows up and turn on the heater, but that soon made the smell impossible to take. So he stopped at a deserted rest area, took everything off but his underwear, and threw all his clothes away, even his boots. The smell was still awful, but at least he could continue driving.

Baughman fretted over what would happen if he was stopped for some reason by a highway patrolman. What would the officer think when he found a foul-smelling man coated from head to foot with tomato juice and wearing only undershorts?

Thankfully, Baughman wasn't stopped by a trooper.

But he was by a flat tire.

Only twenty minutes from home, just as he was breathing easier, thinking he was in the clear . . . BAM! . . . his right rear tire went flat. He coasted to the shoulder of the road and panicked. *What was he going to do now?* he wondered.

But then he remembered the chest-high waders he had in the trunk of the car. He donned them and tackled the tire. A number of cars slowed down to help, but the drivers took a whiff, took a look, and then took off.

With the tire replaced, Baughman finally made it home. But it was two days before he could eat at the dinner table again. And it was two days before the dog stopped backing off whenever his master approached.

Since then Baughman has never sought another skunk tail again.

Who Else Belongs in The Fishing Hall of SHAME™?

Do you have any nominations for The Fishing Hall of SHAME™? Give us your picks of the most shameful, funniest, embarrassing, wackiest, boneheaded moments in sports fishing. Here's your opportunity to pay a lighthearted tribute to the grandest of all outdoor activities.

Please describe your nominations in detail. Those nominations that are documented with the greatest number of facts—such as firsthand accounts or newspaper or magazine clippings—have the best chance of being inducted into The Fishing Hall of SHAME™. Feel free to send as many nominations as you wish. If you don't find an existing category listed in this book, then make up your own category. All submitted material becomes the property of The Fishing Hall of SHAME™ and is nonreturnable. Mail your nominations to:

> The Fishing Hall of SHAME™
> P.O Box 31867
> Palm Beach Gardens, FL 33420